The Faith of a Mockingbird

MATT RAWLE

the faith of a

Mockingbird

A SMALL GROUP STUDY
CONNECTING CHRIST AND CULTURE

Abingdon Press / Nashville

THE FAITH OF A MOCKINGBIRD
A SMALL GROUP STUDY
CONNECTING CHRIST AND CULTURE

For my wife, Christie

CONTENTS

the faith of a

Mockingbird

INTRODUCTION

What comes to mind when you hear someone refer to *pop culture*?

Maybe you think about fast food restaurants or the newest phone apps or the reality television—all things that are seemingly ever-present in our world today. Or maybe your mind tends to drift back to what was most popular when you were a kid. Maybe visions of bell bottoms and disco, or big hair and neon spandex, or flannel shirts and grunge rock dance through your mind.

No matter which decade you were born in, there is no doubt that the "popular culture" of the time—the music, the books, the television, the movies, the media has much to say about the world in which we live. The word *culture* is used often, by many different people in many different ways, but in its simplest form, *culture* is simply an expression of how a community understands itself. God, our Creator, supplies us with the raw ingredients of humanity—talents, time, creativity, desires, ingenuity—and "culture" is whatever we cook up. Stories, songs, recipes, traditions,

9

art, and language are all displays of how we interpret the world and our place in it.

So what role does God play in our culture—in our day-to-day lives and in the work of our hands that produces music and art and literature and plays and movies and technology? Throughout history, people have debated this issue and adamantly drawn a dividing line between that which should be considered "sacred" (that which is explicitly religious in nature) and that which should be considered "secular" (that is, everything else). At first glance, these may be seemingly easy judgments to make, but when we stop to examine what God has to say about this division, we might be surprised at what we find.

Scripture says that *all* things were made through Christ (John 1:3), and through Christ *all* things were reconciled to God (Colossians 1:20). In other words, everything and everyone in our world contains a spark of the divine—everything is sacred, and whether or not we choose to live in that truth depends on our perspective. For example, think of sunlight as a holy (sacred) gift from God. God offers us sunlight so that we can see the world around us. We can celebrate the sacred by creating things that enhance the light in our homes, such as larger windows or skylights, or we can hang heavy drapes and close the shutters in order to diminish the sacred and shut out the light. Our sacred work is letting in as much light as possible, and those things that keep the light out need to be rejected or transformed.

Through Jesus, God put on flesh and walked among us, in order to re-narrate what it means to be a child of God. God assumed culture and transformed it. So now all is sacred, and in everything we are to see and proclaim his glory. I truly believe we are called not to reject the culture we live in, but to re-narrate its meaning—to tell God's story in the midst of it. Jesus didn't reject the Cross (the sin of our world); rather, Jesus accepted it and transformed it from a death instrument into a symbol of life and reconciliation.

THE POP IN CULTURE

Sometimes it's easy to see God in the midst of culture—in the stories of Scripture and in reverent hymns and worshipful icons. Other times the divine is more veiled—hidden in a novel, concealed in classic rock, obscured by an impressionist's palate.

As we walk with Christ, we discover the divine all around us, and in turn, the world invites us into a deeper picture of its Creator. Through this lens of God's redemption story, we are invited to look at culture in a new and inviting way. We are invited to dive into the realms of literature, art, and entertainment to explore and discover how God is working in and through us and in the world around us to tell his great story of redemption.

The Pop in Culture series is a collection of studies about faith and popular culture. Each study uses a work of pop culture as a way to examine questions and issues of the Christian faith. Studies consist of a book, DVD, and leader guide. Our hope and prayer is that the studies will open our eyes to the spiritual truths that exist all around us in books, movies, music, and television.

TO KILL A MOCKINGBIRD

Sin and redemption and wisdom and love are all themes that comprise Harper Lee's masterpiece, *To Kill a Mockingbird*. An influential and transformative work, *To Kill a Mockingbird* is one piece of popular culture that has certainly withstood the test of time. Published in 1960, *To Kill a Mockingbird* serves as a lens through which we can understand our place in the world, how we play a role in God's story, and what it means to live out a hopeful faith in a broken world.

In this study, we will explore the attributes and lives of four of the book's main characters—Scout Finch, Atticus Finch, Tom Robinson, and Boo Radley—and what each can teach us about faith and redemption. Each chapter is divided into five sections, perfect for daily readings, with questions for reflection at the end of each section. We begin with Scout, our narrator, who offers her story as a means of understanding our own. Next we will look at the fascinating character of Atticus Finch, who culturally redefines what it means to be a hero—namely that Christians aren't called to be heroes, but saints. Then we encounter Tom Robinson, who begs us to ask how we can fight the good fight of racial reconciliation. Finally, we will ponder one of the most haunting questions in all of American literature—"Who is Boo Radley?"—and explore how Scout's fascination with Boo can drive our desire to discover our sometimes mysterious Lord.

I have heard it said that the sermon you hear is not nearly as powerful as the sermon you *overhear*, that a direct word spoken with pointed finger is not nearly as provocative, remembered, or convicting as having your ear glued to the wall hearing a muted conversation not meant for you. Studying *To Kill a Mockingbird* combines the best of both worlds. As we read, we are able to live through these timeless characters and hear their pointed words of truth, and we also "overhear" the discoveries of the citizens of Maycomb County as they encounter the prophetic truth of mystery, courage, mercy, and justice.

To Kill a Mockingbird is the story of a broken town, full of broken people, living within a corrupt and broken system; but, like all good stories, redemption waits just around the corner, and beckons us to discover how our own broken lives are part of God's timeless redemption story.

To Kill a Mockingbird

A Quick Refresher

Set in the fictional small town of Maycomb, Alabama, during the Great Depression, Harper Lee's *To Kill a Mockingbird* is considered one of the greatest pieces of American literature. Told through the eyes of Scout, the young daughter of local lawyer Atticus Finch, this coming-of-age story follows Scout and her brother, Jem, as they learn to navigate the colorful and complicated world in which they live.

The novel gives Scout's perspective of the rhythm of Maycomb's daily small-town life, which to her is comfortable and predictable. Raised by their widowed father, Atticus, and their feisty and wise housekeeper, Calpurnia, Jem and Scout's roots are deeply entrenched in their small Alabama town.

The story begins the summer Scout is almost six years old and Jem is nearly ten. The siblings' routine begins its typical rhythm, until Dill, the nephew of a neighbor, arrives for the summer and becomes their constant playmate. Soon the three's childhood curiosity and attention becomes fixated on the eerie, ramshackle house next door, inhabited by Mr. Radley and his mysterious son, Arthur—nicknamed "Boo" by the children, because he has not been seen out of his house for many years and wild rumors swirl around who—or what—he really is. Over the course of a few summers, the group spends most of their time together trying to draw Boo out of the Radley house, to no avail. But when Scout and Jem begin to find little gifts seemingly left for them in the hole of a tree in the Radley yard, they start to wonder if someone hasn't been watching and listening to their games after all.

When Atticus is appointed to defend Tom Robinson, a black man accused of raping a white woman, the Finches' quiet lives are turned upside down. Respected as an honorable and wise man in the county, Atticus accepts the job and commits himself to proving Tom's innocence, an unpopular position to take in the segregated Jim Crow South. Many can't believe that Attitcus would work to defend a black man, and as a result, he and the children begin to feel ostracized from some in the community and are even the subject of taunts and threats.

The drama begins to heighten when the neighborhood rallies together to extinguish a fire at Ms. Maudie's house. This sad event sets the town on edge just before Tom Robinson's trial begins, but it also offers an unexpected opportunity for grace—when Scout returns home after watching the home burn, she realizes that someone had put a blanket around her, and Atticus reveals that she was too busy watching the house to realize that it was the infamous Boo who had reached out to comfort her.

To Kill a Mockingbird's conclusion focuses on Atticus' defense of Tom Robinson and brings to light the evils of systematic racism. As the trial unfolds, Tom's innocence seems clear, but the all-white jury lacks the imagination to see a black man as anything but guilty. Tom is convicted, and later dies during an alleged jailbreak attempt. Atticus' arguments during the trial so offend and anger Bob Ewell, the alleged victim's father, that he vows revenge. One dark autumn night Ewell attacks Jem and Scout as they walk home from a school pageant. His drunken intention is to kill them, and he succeeds in breaking Jem's arm before Boo Radley emerges and steps in to protect the children. Ewell is left dead at the scene. In order to shield the reclusive Boo from any unwanted attention, Sheriff Heck Tate emphatically concludes that Bob Ewell fell on his own knife during the struggle, and the matter is closed, with no one else involved.

The book's title, *To Kill a Mockingbird*, stems from a comment Atticus makes to the children as Jem is learning to shoot his air rifle. Atticus tells Jem not to shoot any mockingbirds, that it would be a sin to do that. Noting that as the only time she ever heard Atticus say something was a sin, Scout asks Ms. Maudie what Atticus meant; and Ms. Maudie says that mockingbirds don't cause any harm to anyone, so they should be left alone to live in peace. At the end of the novel, Scout realizes that Boo is like a mockingbird, and to expose him to public curiosity and scrutiny would be unfair to him. With Sheriff Tate's simple act of grace, Scout understands that even in the midst of cruelty and hate, goodness remains.

the faith of a

Mockingbird

Chapter One

SCOUT FINCH
TELLING YOUR STORY

There are different spiritual gifts but the same Spirit; and there are different ministries and the same Lord; and there are different activities but the same God who produces all of them in everyone. – 1 Corinthians 12:4–6

*H*ave you ever returned to your childhood elementary school and marveled at how everything is smaller than you remembered? When I was in the third grade, the cafeteria seemed wide as a great hall, the outside doors were as heavy as fortified castle walls, and the principal's desk was a grand altar. Of course, I see things differently now. When I go back there, the ceilings are lower, the doorways more narrow, the desks and sinks miniature versions of the real thing. I can hardly squeeze into the plastic cafeteria seats. Those fortified entry doors are now propped open with a small wooden triangle, allowing a new generation of children to invade the hallways. And the principal's desk . . . well, okay, it still looks like an altar.

To Kill a Mockingbird is Scout's story, told through her childhood perspective of the world around her. Some of her memories are simple: steamy summer afternoons playing with friends, early evening dinners with family, classroom struggles with teachers who just don't understand. Other memories are more difficult: her father leaving home late at night to protect the prisoner inside the Maycomb jail, the seemingly ordained difference between blacks and whites, the way an innocent man such as Tom Robinson could be ruled guilty. Then there are the memories that are mysterious, memories that Scout seems almost reluctant to share, such as those involving the haunting figure of Boo Radley.

We too carry memories. Some are easy to recall, trivial, and superficial. Other memories lead us to consider an alternate reality, asking "What if?" Scout's story reminds us that, over time, our understanding of the world changes. The grade-school water fountains are not nearly so tall, and unrequited love doesn't bring about the end of the world. Scout has her story, we have ours, and both are changing as we grow.

Did you ever think that God has a story too? It's the story of life, and all of us are part of it—growing, changing, helping in our own small ways to determine what will happen next. In this book of reflections, we'll talk about the story Scout tells in *To Kill a Mockingbird*. If we pay attention, maybe we'll learn something about our own stories and, ultimately, about God's great story of faith, love, and sacrifice.

MEET SCOUT FINCH

To Kill a Mockingbird's narrator, "Scout" Finch, is a young girl mature beyond her years, with a sharp intellect and a tongue to match. Born Jean Louis Finch, Scout's mother died from a sudden heart attack when she was just two years old and her older brother, Jem, was six. After her mother's death, the children's raising fell to their father, Atticus, along with the support of the family cook, Calpurnia, who eagerly keeps the children in line.

Raised to be intelligent and reasonable, Scout is smart as a whip and has been able to read for as long as she can remember, but she often lets her passions get the best of her. Scout doesn't fit the stereotype of a prim and proper young lady of the Deep South—when offended or taunted by a bully, she's more likely to let her fists do the talking than to speak a polite word. When her friend Dill promises to marry her one day, but then ignores her, wanting to play with Jem more than her, Scout just can't help but rough him up a little for it.

Scout's world revolves around her home and family. She adores her father and has a strong bond with her brother, though the two siblings have their fair share of arguments and certainly find lots of ways to get into trouble together. The confidence and affection she receives at home give Scout wisdom beyond her years, but her simple, childlike way of understanding her world makes her voice unique and powerful. She's not afraid to ask the tough questions, keeping the adults around her constantly on their toes.

Scout's Story

"When he was nearly thirteen, my brother Jem got his arm badly broken at the elbow."[1] — Scout

Whether or not you have read Harper Lee's Pulitzer Prize–winning novel, *To Kill a Mockingbird,* or have seen the Academy Award–winning movie starring Gregory Peck, a brief overview of the story quickly reveals that it connects deeply at a heart level. It is the story of a young girl, Scout, and her older brother, Jem, growing up in the fictional Southern town of Maycomb, Alabama. Scout narrates her preadolescent journey through the difficulty of the Great Depression and the confusing and systemic racism pervasive in the Jim Crow South.

Much of Scout's story reflects characters and events from Lee's own history as a young girl growing up in Monroeville, Alabama. Lee's father was a lawyer, which offered her great insight in crafting the character of Scout's father, Atticus Finch. The climax of the story, the trial of Tom Robinson, is reminiscent of the 1931 trial of nine African American men in Scottsboro, Alabama, in which five of the nine men received lengthy prison terms that many suggested were the result of racial prejudice. Lee's own reflections about growing up in the 1930s South created the framework for Scout's narrative, a story that challenges each of us to reflect on our own stories. The various characters in *To Kill a Mockingbird* invite us to consider how we each understand our place in the world, how we play a role in God's story, and what it means to live out a hopeful faith in a broken world. The book begins with Scout recalling the time Jem broke his arm, though we don't find out how that actually happens until the final scenes of the book.

Brokenness frames the entire story of *Mockingbird* in much the same way that brokenness is central to the Christian faith—Jesus' body was broken on the cross for our sin, and it is through his life, suffering, death, and resurrection that we have access to God's grace. I was reminded of this one Sunday when, before our church's worship time, a woman met me in the back of the sanctuary. She confessed that she had lost hope because her failing body was causing her almost constant pain. After I invited her to sit, we held hands for prayer and briefly talked about how our church could meet her needs. Near the end of the service, during Holy Communion, this now-tearful woman came to our prayer station. We again held hands as she offered another confession. She said, "Forgive me. When you broke the bread at the table, I realized for the first time in my life that salvation is offered through a broken body, not one that is whole. Though my health is failing, my hope has been restored." Through Jesus' brokenness and resurrection, our severed relationship with God is mended and made whole.

Early in *To Kill a Mockingbird,* Scout describes her father, Atticus, in simple and broad strokes, revealing him to be a man of great character and selflessness. As Scout's story grows, so do her memories of Atticus. We first experience Atticus through his profound parental poise, answering Scout's pointed questions with timeless wisdom about the importance of defending the defenseless and making an effort to really understand another person from his or her point of view. As the story continues, Atticus as a father figure gives way to Atticus the Civil Rights saint. Watching Tom Robinson's trial from the "Colored" balcony, Scout remembers Reverend Sykes asking her to stand in figurative salute with the rest of Maycomb's African American residents as Atticus walks the lonely aisle at the end of the trial.

It is interesting that Scout had to be encouraged to stand as a show of respect for Atticus, but then we remember that, from Scout's perspective, Atticus was simply her father; and it reminds me that the way we see the world affects the stories we tell. Consider the complementary pictures of God in the Bible's two creation accounts. In Genesis 1, God is revealed in his power. God speaks and things happen. Humanity is mentioned only briefly, which emphasizes God's almighty status. Genesis 2 reveals a more human creator, a God who kneels down in the dirt, fashions people from the clay, and walks with them in the garden. Those in the court-house balcony stood with a kind of holy reverence toward Atticus; but Scout remained crouched, not out of irreverence, but because her Atticus was a bit more down-to-earth. He was someone who was a constant presence in her life, who loved her, disciplined her, and cared for her daily needs. She loved him not because of his noble courage, but because he was her father.

Though our God is the Creator of the universe, almighty and omnipotent and worthy of our reverent praise, he is also our ever-present Father, tenderly caring for us in our daily needs. And he is the One who takes our brokenness and redeems it, giving us a hope that only he can give and writing our stories as only he can.

Can you think of a time in your life where brokenness led to healing?

What does it mean to you that we can find wholeness through Jesus' brokenness?

How do you view your relationship with God the Father, who is at once both almighty and intimate? How has that contradiction colored your own story?

Four Portraits

Again, the high priest asked, "Are you the Christ, the Son of the blessed one?" – Mark 14:61b

We each understand our place in the world in different ways. If Jem were our *Mockingbird* narrator, the characters would look slightly different. Hope in the midst of brokenness would still be the narrative truth; but because of their life experiences, Jem and Scout would differ in how they understand brokenness. Instead of a broken arm, Jem's story might have begun with the death of his mother, a mother Scout hardly remembers. It is as fitting for Scout to diminish her mother's death as it would be for Jem to be consumed by it. Similarly, the person sitting across the table from you has a personal story with different peaks and valleys, affecting how he or she understands the world. But our stories are not so different that goodness is completely relative. For instance, we might disagree about which ice cream flavor is best—you might picture a scoop of vanilla and my cup might be filled with chocolate, or maybe your favorite flavor is pistachio because your grandmother made it during the holidays (surely the only reason someone would ever prefer it)—but we would probably all agree that ice cream is good.

Scripture offers us a foundation for appreciating the beauty and importance of differing perspectives. The New Testament, for example, provides at least four different portraits of Jesus. Mark, the oldest Gospel, presents a Jesus who is fast moving and mysterious. Jesus appears out of nowhere with no story of his birth, and he

DID YOU KNOW?

To Kill a Mockingbird, published in 1960, was Harper Lee's only novel until 2015, when her second novel, *Go Set a Watchman,* was scheduled for release.

exits with only an empty tomb (sort of). If Mark's Jesus appears as a mysterious miracle worker, Matthew's Jesus looks a lot like Moses. Jesus travels in and out of Egypt to escape Herod's slaughter. Jesus preaches from the mountaintop and renarrates the law. Jesus' actions are loosely divided into five sections, reminding the reader of the five books of Moses. Luke, by contrast, presents a more Gentile-friendly Jesus. Jesus preaches not from a mountaintop but on a level place, suggesting a great passion for social justice. In Luke, Jesus describes the cup of wine at the Passover meal as the "new covenant," where Matthew and Mark show nothing new about it. And then John's picture of Jesus is altogether different and his actions follow a different timeline. Just as Jesus' humanity is emphasized in Luke, his divinity is portrayed in John, where Jesus dances with imagery and metaphor, exchanges bread and wine for a basin of water and dirty feet, and is crucified before the Passover meal instead of after, as described in the other three Gospels.

I'll never forget the time I realized all these different versions of the Gospels existed. It was Holy Week my junior year of high school when I started really reading the Bible for myself; and as I sat in my bedroom late one night, reading Mark's account of Jesus' trial, I read about when Caiaphas asked Jesus if he was the Messiah. Jesus replied, "I am," which seems to be a pretty straightforward answer. For fun I turned to Matthew to read his account of Jesus' trial and was surprised by what I found. In Matthew, Caiaphas asks the same question, but curiously Jesus responds differently: "You have said so." I sat thinking to myself, "Why has no one mentioned this to me?" I next turned to Luke's Gospel, which shows yet a third answer, and to John, whose account is altogether different. In that moment, Scripture became invitingly complex to me. The Gospels offered me four different windows into Jesus' identity, and I felt the Holy Spirit encouraging me to share my discovery with anyone who would listen.

So, whose Gospel picture of Jesus is the correct one? All of them! The key lies in perspective. Even though the Holy Spirit inspired all four of the Gospel authors, each had his own unique perspective. It reminds us that we each experience God in a unique way, and each of us plays a particular role in telling God's story. Is there a story from Jesus' life that resonates with you? Do his healings call you to serve the sick? Does his feeding of the five thousand call you to start a food ministry? Do his parables encourage you to become a teacher? If you look, you'll no doubt find yourself in the gospel story.

Our differing perspectives point us to the truth that can be found in the space between where my experience ends and yours begins. Scout's memory of Tom Robinson's trial, which occupies much of her story, shows us how elusive the truth can be. Is Tom really being honest? Is Bob Ewell trying to hide something? Does Atticus believe Tom is not guilty, or is he simply trying to win a case? Why does the jury unquestionably believe one person's word over another's?

In Scout's account, Atticus returns home after the trial to find the kitchen overflowing with food from Maycomb's appreciative black community. He has lost the trial, but his work is met with an abundance of thanksgiving. Is he a loser or a saint? The truth is in the space between. When our differing viewpoints with others make the truth difficult to see, the best response is thanksgiving for those places where we *do* find the truth—in the free gift of each breath, in the consistent beauty of a sunrise, in the power and grace of a handshake or a hug, in standing up for those who cannot stand.

Where or how do you see God's truth being revealed in your own life?

Is there a particular portrait of Jesus in the Bible that resonates with you? Why?

For what do you give thanks?

FINDING YOUR PLACE

There are different spiritual gifts but the same Spirit; and there are different ministries and the same Lord; and there are different activities but the same God who produces all of them in everyone. – 1 Corinthians 12:4–6

Discovering and living out our place in God's story is a means of celebrating the truth, even if it is sometimes difficult to discern. Early in *To Kill a Mockingbird,* Scout finds it difficult to fit in. Her new first grade teacher, Miss Caroline Fisher, doesn't understand her. Scout gets into fights on the playground. She asks adults difficult questions they don't want to answer. She doesn't mind her own business, and Maycomb doesn't know what to do with people who don't know their place. Little girls are to wear dresses and remain quiet. Little boys are to mind their fathers and stay out of trouble. Men go to work. Women stay at home, unless they choose to teach or nurse. White folk go here. Black folk stay there. Everyone has her or his neat and predictable place—and then there is Scout.

What do you consider to be your "place" in life? Were you told where to fit in, or were you invited into a particular role? All God's creatures have a place in the choir; the question is, "Who assigns the parts?" One thing I quickly learned when I became a parent was that my life was no longer my own. I could not believe the hospital let us go home with a new human being without some kind of instruction manual or professional assistant to guide us. The shift from spouse to parent is dramatic and swift. There were late-night feedings, early-morning diaper changes, the minivan purchase . . . it was a very different way of life. "Parent" was a new and demanding role to play. The baby didn't put me in my place or tell me what I should or shouldn't be doing; rather parenthood was simply a new chapter of life. It is a blessing, though nowhere in Scripture does it say all blessings are easy to swallow! The same holds true when a child has to take care of an ailing parent, and the seemingly natural relationship roles are reversed. It can be difficult to understand one's new place in a new world. This is especially true in times of great loss. There is little way to prepare for the role of a childless parent or grieving spouse.

What daily role do you play? Is it constant or ever changing? Who assigned your part? Sometimes society assigns the roles we play, both for good and for ill. Even in small-town, Depression-era Maycomb, Alabama, there is a definitive line between those who are in and those who are out. During the first week of school, when Ms. Fisher notices that Walter Cunningham has no money for lunch, she tries to offer him a loan; but the young, terribly thin child refuses. Scout announces to Ms. Fisher that Walter is a Cunningham, thinking that knowledge of his name would offer a clue to his status. Ms. Fisher's confusion is the catalyst of Scout's explicit explanation that the Cunninghams are poor and will always be poor. Scout's helpful advice is met with a ruler rap to the back of the hand, so at the end of the day she decides to rub Walter's face in the dirt as payment. Seeing Walter's public shaming, Jem insists that Walter join them for dinner. Walter's dining habits are peculiar, and when Scout raises her voice in protest, Calpurnia, the Finches' housekeeper, reminds Scout that any guest at the table is "company," and in the South, there is no more-revered status.

Walter's invitation to the Finches' table breaks down Maycomb society's clearly defined roles. Walter, the outsider, is welcomed to the table of hospitality. The last becomes first, and the humble is exalted (see Matthew 20:16). The gospel of Jesus is the story of outsiders being welcomed in. Those who walk with Jesus are fishermen who haven't caught anything, a woman who was suffering for twelve years, a pessimist who thinks nothing good can come from Nazareth, a woman at a well who knows the pain of divorce, and a zealot who wants to overthrow the government. Jesus looks to all of them, takes bread, breaks the bread, offers it to them and says that it is his body broken so that they have a place at the table.

There are many narratives in this world that tell us who and what we are supposed to be, where we are supposed to go, and where our place ought to be. But the only invitation that truly matters is the seat Christ offers at his table of bread and wine, a place of holy communion where all are welcome to receive God's grace and share peace with one another.

How do you understand the roles you are playing right now? Who assigned those roles to you?

Read 1 Corinthians 12:4–11. What role does Scripture assign you?

How does your community of faith welcome and invite those on the margins? Who do you need to welcome to your table so that the gospel might come alive for them?

WASH, RINSE, AND REPEAT

> *Rejoice always. Pray continually. Give thanks in every situation because this is God's will for you in Christ Jesus.*
> *— 1 Thessalonians 5:16–18*

Have you ever noticed some of the strange directions printed on common household products? Something like, "Step one: Remove product from packaging," or "Caution: After heating in the microwave, the product you are about to enjoy will be hot." It seems silly to have to say, "First, turn the power button to the On position," but sometimes you just have to be specific.

My sister recently noticed that her daughter's showers were lasting a very long time. She didn't think anything of it at first, but eventually, when her showers had crossed the forty-five-minute mark, she finally knocked on the door and asked, "Dear, what's taking so long?"

"I'm still washing my hair," was the reply.

Twenty minutes later, when her now hour-long shower had used up all of the hot water, my sister asked, "Why did it take you so long to wash your hair?"

My niece replied, "The bottle said, 'Wash, rinse, and repeat,' so I did, until the water turned cold."

If culture is simply what we make of the world,[2] then culture is born through repetition. *Wash, rinse, repeat.* Hearing about Scout's daily routine gives us a glimpse of what she values and what is important to her and her family. For instance, every evening before going to bed Scout and Atticus read together. It is simply part of their daily rhythm, and therefore part of who Scout is, which is why she maintains that she has been able to read since birth. That's how rooted in identity a daily habit can become.

Scout's life is full of simple habits and habitual honesty. Every afternoon, she meets her father at the end of the street and walks home with him, eats dinner with her family, and then sits in her father's lap to hear a good book. These habits give birth to a habitual honesty in her relationship with Atticus. Her relationship with her father is such that her questions to him are offered with an unfiltered, childlike honesty that violates the common sensibilities of most of the other adults in her life. She asks pointedly, "Do you defend Negros?" and "Why does that man pay you in vegetables?" and "Are we poor?"

One Valentine's Day several years ago one of my daughters and I went to a local Chinese restaurant for take-out. As I pulled into the parking lot, she asked, "Daddy, are Mimi and Paw-Paw going to die?"

I just wanted to pick up some egg rolls, but I took a deep breath and entertained her question with trepidation. I'm a pastor—I should have had this answer in the bag, but I knew how my daughter poured over every word, so I knew the words had to be chosen wisely.

"Well, yes, sweetie," I said. "Everything that is born dies one day."

I turned off the ignition and unbuckled the seat belt, mildly gloating over my success as a pastor/father, when she started to cry.

"But, sweetie," I said, "there's good news. When we die we get to live with God in heaven."

She cried even louder. "But I don't want Mimi and Paw-Paw to live with God in heaven. I want them to live down here with us."

Wonderful, I thought. *My romantic Valentine's Day Chinese take-out is getting cold, and I am destroying my daughter's faith all in the same sitting.*

Then, in a flash—thank you, Holy Spirit!—I said, "What do we pray every night before going to bed?"

"The Lord's Prayer," she answered.

"That's right. In the Lord's Prayer we pray, 'Thy kingdom come, thy will be done on earth as it is in heaven.' You see, dear, God wants heaven and earth to be one and the same thing. One day heaven and earth will be one. So we will live with Mimi and Paw-Paw and God all at the same time."

She seemed satisfied at that, so we got out of the car to pick up our meal and head home. Later, as we pulled into the driveway, my daughter asked, "Daddy, are Mimi and Paw-Paw going to die before April?"

AND THE AWARD GOES TO . . .

The film version of *To Kill a Mockingbird* was nominated for eight Academy Awards in 1963. Gregory Peck was nominated and won for Best Actor. The film also won Best Art Direction and Best Screenplay.

Suddenly this whole question-and-answer session made sense—
Mimi and Paw-Paw had planned a grandkids' trip to Disney World
for the week after Easter. My daughter wasn't interested in a deep
theological discussion of the afterlife—she wanted to know if
"earth" would remain long enough for her to see Mickey Mouse.

Children often ask difficult questions. It's not that the questions
are complicated; rather their questions are framed within an honesty
adults have forgotten how to use. We grown-ups can become overly
concerned with appearances, status, gesturing, and posturing, and
so the simple questions of children can offend our sensibilities.
But sometimes our sensibilities need offending. As a Christian
community, it is important to ask the difficult questions: Why does
abject poverty still exist? Why does America, a nation built on the
ideals of freedom, lead the world in adult incarcerations? Why do
women receive less salary on the dollar than men? Why is the Super
Bowl the greatest sex-trafficking event the world has ever known?
Why do some denominations fight over who can get married, but
they do not openly grieve when marriages are broken?

Are you shifting in your seat yet? These are questions that do
not have easy answers, and they are painted with broad strokes of
assumptions on both sides of a sensible divide. But have we lost our
courage to even ask the hard questions?

"What is rape?" Scout asks her father one evening. He frankly
replies, "Carnal knowledge of a female by force and without
consent."[3] Sometimes there is a straightforward answer to a question;
other times truth telling is more complex. Some live according to
"The truth is the truth, and lying is lying," mantra, but truth telling
goes over and above the simple conveyance of facts. For example,
if I am harboring Jews in my home, and a Nazi officer comes to
the door and asks if I am hiding any Jews, I'm going to lie and
say no. Does this mean I am bearing a false witness in violation

of the Ten Commandments? No, because truth is that which is life giving. Truth is not bound by the conveyance of fact; rather it is the proclamation of what brings life. It is the proclamation of Resurrection. Truth is the awareness that poverty, hate, inequality, and death exist, but it is also the liberating wakefulness that none of these are powerful enough to overcome the life-giving power of Jesus' resurrection—the proof that God's word can be trusted.

Our habits become the tools we use to understand what God is doing in the world and what our role in that work is. Habits are the means of grace whereby we experience God's merciful and loving will, because the rhythm and daily structure of habitual love offers us the courage and compassion to embrace the truth so that we can wash the world in the waters of baptism, to rinse away that which separates us from God and from each other, and repeat until Jesus returns. Because being in Christ is not about definitions but discernment. Being in Christ is not about who is in and who is out, but how those on the outside might be welcomed in with trans- formative hospitality. Being in Christ means we ask the difficult questions, that we look at our own prejudices and remember how Jesus responded to an outsider:

> Jesus turned to the woman and said to Simon, "Do you see this woman? When I entered your home, you didn't give me water for my feet, but she wet my feet with tears and wiped them with her hair. You didn't greet me with a kiss, but she hasn't stopped kissing my feet since I came in. You didn't anoint my head with oil, but she has poured perfumed oil on my feet. This is why I tell you that her many sins have been forgiven; so she has shown great love. The one who is forgiven little loves little."
>
> Then Jesus said to her, "Your sins are forgiven."
>
> (Luke 7:44–48)

Spending our time in ministry with the poor, clothing the naked, and communing at an open table begin to change who we are and who we perceive our neighbor to be. If our culture is an expression of what we wash, rinse, and repeat, may our culture be a reflection of habitual love.

What do your daily habits reveal about who you are? Is there a daily habit you can't imagine not having?

How do your daily habits reveal your faith and values?

Read Galatians 5:22–23 and 1 Thessalonians 5:16–18. What do they tell us about life-giving habits we should form in our lives?

MAKING ROOM FOR AWE AND WONDER

"She was the bravest person I ever knew."[4]
—Atticus, on Mrs. Dubose

As Scout and Jem walk home from school every day, they have to pass the house of the elderly Mrs. Dubose, who is in the habit of yelling insults at them as they walk by. Committed to bearing these daily tirades, Scout and Jem's predictable daily schedule is interrupted when Jem snaps one day and hacks down all of the ornery old lady's camellia bushes. Atticus sends Jem over to her house to apologize, and upon returning, Jem reveals that his punishment is that Mrs. Dubose wants him to read to her daily after school for two hours for a whole month.

So every day Jem reads to Mrs. Dubose until the timer in the kitchen sounds, but each day the time seems to stretch longer and longer, until the children are there until well after dark. Later, not long after Jem's punishment is served, Mrs. Dubose dies; and Jem and Scout discover that the lengthening timer was a means by which Mrs. Dubose was working to kick a morphine addiction. It was a habit that she was determined to end before she died, and Jem's reading had served to distract her thoughts during fits of withdrawal.

Habits can have a dark side, and if we aren't careful, our habits can become confining, leaving us with little room for awe or wonder or surprise. One of my good friends often reminds me that we worship a God whose middle name is "Surprise." But sometimes our habits or addictions can get in the way of our relationship with God, confusing how we hear God's story and share God's narrative in the world. When Paul describes a life lived solely under the law in Romans 7, he sounds like he's describing addiction. He writes, "I do not understand my own actions. For I do not do what I want, but I do the very thing I hate" (Romans 7:15 NRSV). No one wakes in the morning wanting to betray trust or destroy relationships, but bad habits can become idols, replacing God's story in our lives, extinguishing our ability to imagine where God is calling.

We miss God's surprising and life-giving spirit when we fall back on destructive habits. When habits go too far, we can become convinced that everything is under our control, that everything can be known and expected. In other words, habits can give rise to false assumptions and unfortunate stereotypes, habits of which we are often not aware. One Sunday morning Scout and her older brother, Jem, went to church with their caretaker, Calpurnia. Scout noticed an immediate difference between her expectation and the reality that was First Purchase African Methodist Episcopal Church. Named "First Purchase" because it was the first purchase made by freed slaves, the sanctuary lacked the usual church affects like an organ, hymnals, or a bulletin. Scout was particularly troubled when Zeebo, Calpurnia's son, rose to lead the singing without the aid of any hymnals; and yet, miraculously (as Scout remembers) the community sang together on pitch from beginning to end. She said at the conclusion of their singing that if she hadn't heard it, she wouldn't have believed it. Shaking her assumptions and habits opened up Scout's imagination to the point where she was bursting with questions, an experience that helped her better understand her place in the unfolding narrative.

If we never have an opportunity to shake our assumptions about how we understand God in the world, even our worship will leave us spiritually sedated. Regardless of whether you enjoy a contemporary or traditional style of worship, there is probably a regular order of worship in your church each and every week. When I was an undergraduate, every Wednesday evening my friends and I would gather for worship at the LSU Wesley Foundation on Chimes Street. Each week we would stand in a circle, reciting The Lord's Prayer to close Holy Communion. One week I was standing next to a fellow student, Chad, who was saying The Lord's Prayer in a Scottish accent. I found it to be jarring, immature, and downright rude, and later I asked him what was up with the sudden urge to be Scottish. He replied that he changed the way he said The Lord's Prayer each week to remind himself to truly listen to the words so that the prayer would never become a meaningless practice.

Worship is an expression of how God is calling your community to participate in Christ's redemptive work. Your liturgy, your work as a worshiping community, is a manifestation of your role in God's

NEXT-DOOR INSPIRATION

The character of Dill was based on writer Truman Capote, who as a child came to live with his aunts in a home next door to Harper Lee. Capote and Lee were longtime friends.

story. Worship is a great habit, but if it becomes monotonous, it can quickly become meaningless. One way to discourage shallow routine is to periodically ask why worship flows the way it does. When Scout heard the First Purchase congregation singing without hymnals, she exploded with questions. When was the last time worship left you dumb with inquisitive awe? Changing our habits can offer us room to ask questions about identity and the way things are so that we can be filled with a holy curiosity about what God is doing in the world.

Sometimes even good habits need to be interrupted or broken all together. In Mark 5, Jesus meets Jairus, a leader of the synagogue, who comes and falls down at Jesus' feet, saying, "My daughter is about to die. Please, come and place your hands on her so that she can be healed and live." So Jesus goes with him. On the way there a large crowd gathers to see what is happening, and Jesus is interrupted by a touch. A woman from the crowd, who had been ill for twelve years—who had tried everything, and paid all kinds of healers to the point of poverty—reached up and touched his cloak.

Jesus stopped and said, "Who touched me?"

One of the disciples said, "What do you mean, 'Who touched you?' Don't you see this crowd? How can you ask such a silly question?"

But the woman came forward and told Jesus everything, and Jesus said, "Daughter, your faith has made you well. Go in peace, and be healed of your disease."

Can you think of a time when your day was interrupted, but it was an interruption that changed your life for the better? Maybe it was the time you stopped everything to answer that phone call, or the late-running meeting that led to a new friendship, or the unexpected time you got to reconnect with someone over coffee. While holy habits sanctify the pieces of our soul, sometimes the breaking of habits brings the pieces together in a way that is life-giving. Sometimes interruptions are the cracks in the wall that allow the living water of the Holy Spirit to come in and mess up our lives for all the right reasons.

What interruptions in your own life have been life giving?

Are there habits in your life that need breaking? What about communal habits in the life of your faith community?

When was the last time God surprised you? Do you think you might surprise God?

Chapter Two

ATTICUS FINCH
WHEN YOUR STORY IS CHALLENGED

Happy are people whose lives are harassed because they are
righteous, because the kingdom of heaven is theirs.

— *Matthew 5:10*

For anyone who has seen the film version of *To Kill a Mockingbird*, it is difficult to think of Atticus Finch as anyone other than Gregory Peck. Peck's distinctive voice and humble bravado so capture Lee's Atticus that even as I read Atticus' closing arguments, Peck's voice overpowers my own imagination. Far be it for me to claim that a movie is better than a book, but I am unsure how one might improve on Peck's performance in this film. His fatherly charm, steadfast resolve, and unruffled composure almost trick the audience into thinking that Atticus is real. Some even argue that Peck is so commanding that what is Scout's story on the pages of Lee's book truly transforms into Atticus' story on the silver screen.

MEET ATTICUS FINCH

Atticus Finch is the moral backbone of Maycomb County, well respected for his intellect, kindness, and polite manner fitting of a Southern gentleman. Atticus' roots run deep in Maycomb County, with the pre–Civil War arrival of his English ancestor, Simon Finch, described as a "fur-trapping apothecary from Cornwall." Generations upon generations of Finches had resided on the cotton farm of Finch's Landing, just east of Maycomb, as had Atticus until he left for law school. His brother, Uncle Jack, also left to become a doctor, and their sister, Alexandra, married and stayed on the land. Because of the family's long-standing residence in the area, Atticus is related, by blood or marriage, to almost every family in town.

After he was elected to the state legislature, Atticus met and married a much younger woman from Montgomery, and their children, Jem and Scout, were born before she died suddenly. From the reader's perspective, Atticus is a model parent. He is fair, exceptionally patient, witty, and religiously educates his children on how to treat others with respect and kindness. The wise advice he gives his children forms the backbone of the central messages of the novel.

Atticus is loved by all until the day he is appointed to defend Tom Robinson, a black man accused of raping a white woman. Atticus believes in Tom's innocence and therefore commits to give him the best defense possible, no matter Tom's race. For some, he is a noble savior. To others he is a traitor. The case becomes the foundation for an indictment of systematic racism in the Jim Crow–era South. The difficult job of speaking truth, his fatherly compassion, and wise sayings paint Atticus as the savior figure in the midst of a town that needs saving.

Whether in film or on folio, the character of Atticus Finch demands our attention for all the right reasons. Atticus is a successful lawyer, loving father, and moral compass for the community. Atticus is beloved because he represents a cultural best. He is committed to nonviolence, using words to maintain control. He maintains a successful career while also making time for his children. He is well respected in the community while stretching the community's imagination for justice. Essentially Atticus is a superhero who fights for truth, justice, and the American Way.

What endears us to superheroes isn't their commitment to the good; rather it is their ability to overcome adversity while maintaining a consistent moral code. Atticus knows that he is going to lose Tom's case, but he fully embraces Tom's defense anyway; and his commitment to justice comes at a price for him and his family—Jem and Scout are mocked at school, Atticus is spat upon, and the family becomes a target of revenge. Atticus represents what it means to fall upward—to lose well. Ultimately Atticus models the Christian ethics of strength through sacrifice and victory as defeat, a way of life rooted in Christ's suffering, death, and resurrection. His example prompts us to reflect on our own commitment—it may be easy to follow Christ when things go well, but are we willing to follow Christ's footsteps even when they lead to the cross?

THE POWER OF WORDS

"'Good evening, Mrs. Dubose! You look like a picture this evening.'
I never heard Atticus say like a picture of what."[1]—*Scout*

The words we speak and share with one another are windows into how we understand the world and our place in it. To say that Atticus Finch has a gift for words would be an understatement. His speeches about the importance of compromise and about the significance of walking around in someone else's skin in order to really understand them ring as true today and are as universal as when Lee first wrote them. These moral expressions shine a light on who Atticus is and how he understands his place in the world. He is committed to understanding the other person's point of view. He believes in the great equalizer of the justice system. He trusts in human goodness and integrity, even when it is difficult to find.

What words regularly flow from your lips? Do your words flow from a place of thanksgiving? Or are your words consumed with suspicion of who the next enemy might be? Words have a profound influence on how we understand who we are and our place in the world. Words are so powerful that everything was created through them. In the beginning of it all, God spoke creation into being. God said, "Let there be," and it was. The Gospel of John begins with remembering that the Word of God was always present with God— begotten, eternal, and ever-present. John continues, "Everything came into being through the Word, and without the Word nothing

42

came into being" (John 1:3). The love that was bound within God's heart took on shape and form once the words "Let there be" were spoken.

The same holds true with the words we speak. Words like, "I love you," "I will always be there for you," or "I do" manifest relationships and transform lives. Likewise, "It's cancer," "I never loved you," or "I'm sorry, there's nothing we could do" change the course of how we understand our identity and place in the world.

Words have power. Words make things real, so it should give us great pause to reflect on the kind of reality we create each day with our words. Does your day begin with words of thanksgiving? Or does your day begin with a heavy sigh as your open your e-mail? Maybe your day begins with someone else's words—"Mommy, I'm up!" Perhaps it's the end of the day when our words matter most. During the six days of creation, God spoke just before evening, offering rest as creation's first job. Maybe those words we speak to our children before bed are the most important? Maybe the words spoken to a lover just before the lights go out are the words that remain? Perhaps our daily words should always be understood as our last. Maybe speaking only the words we want to be remembered for can do more good in the world than any doctrinal debate.

Atticus seems to understand that those last-heard words are the ones that leave a lasting impression. One evening, just before bed, Scout overhears Atticus talking to Uncle Jack about Tom Robinson's case. Atticus laments that there's little hope of winning the case, but his hope is that he might get Jem and Scout to adulthood without them catching Maycomb's "usual disease" of racism, bitterness, and hate. Atticus says to Uncle Jack that he hopes Jem and Scout come to him for answers rather than relying on the collective experience of the town. He then calls up to Scout, telling her to go to bed. A surprised Scout wonders how Atticus knew she was listening, but

---

LASTING BONDS

Gregory Peck (Atticus) and Brock Peters (Tom Robinson) formed a friendship during the filming of the movie and remained such close friends that Peters gave Peck's eulogy when he died in 2003.

---

as she recalls the story later, she realizes Atticus had wanted her to hear every word that night.

Atticus' words are powerful, but their power rests not in forcefulness or control. When God created, God used words of permission rather than power. God looked at the formless void and said, "Let there be;" and "Let there be" is quite different from "There shall be." God creates through permission. God allows the waters to bring forth swarming creatures. God allows the earth to produce vegetation and creeping things. God's words are powerful not because of forced limitation. God's words are powerful because of their unbound potential and invitation. God invites creation to participate in its own formation. When Atticus speaks to the jury, he is not telling them what to think or what to believe; rather, he is inviting them to imagine a different, more hopeful way. Atticus can shape and mold the imagination because he understands the secret of words' power—integrity.

Words are only as powerful as the speaker's integrity. "We should all be one" sounds like the gospel when Jesus says it. It means something completely different if Lex Luthor says it. It may be true that actions speak louder than words, but it is certainly true that words receive their power through the action of the speaker. Jesus said:

> "You have heard that it was said to those who lived long ago: Don't make a false solemn pledge, but you should follow

through on what you have pledged to the Lord. But I say to you that you must not pledge at all. You must not pledge by heaven, because it's God's throne. You must not pledge by earth, because it's God's footstool. You must not pledge by Jerusalem, because it's the city of the great king. And you must not pledge by your head, because you can't turn one hair white or black. Let your *yes* mean yes, and your *no* mean no. Anything more than this comes from the evil one." (Matthew 5:33–37)

During the time Jesus lived, a person's word was a legal contract. In order to seal a contract, you would swear on something, like putting something up for collateral. You might say something such as, "I swear on my house that I am telling the truth." In other words, if you were caught being deceitful, you would surrender your home. In these situations you would create rules of how to transfer property in case you broke your promise. You would put together a big book of discipline to outline how to handle the issue if rules were broken. Jesus is saying that we should not swear at all, meaning that there is no need to create laws to figure out what to do when a promise is broken because, as Christians, we shouldn't break our promises. "Let your *yes* mean yes, and your *no* mean no" (Matthew 5:37).

Our words are only as powerful as the integrity behind them. When Atticus speaks with his children, with the jury, and with the people of Maycomb, his words carry weight. It's not that his words are demanding or threatening, but they rest on the foundation of his moral character, a character that invites the hearer to imagine a new way, to believe that goodness and peace are real and necessary and available within everyone. His words echo the permissive "Let there be," which brought forth everything that is. Words not only reveal how we understand who we are and the world around us, but they are also a gift that invites others to understand who God is calling them to be.

Whose words matter in your life? Who do you find to be full of integrity?

Do your words tend to be more inviting (Let there be) or more controlling (Thou shall not)?

What have you not said today that needed to be said? How will you say it tomorrow?

MORE THAN A COMPROMISE

Jesus answered, "I am the way, the truth, and the life. No one comes to the Father except through me. – John 14:6

Atticus seems to say all the right things at all the right times. One afternoon Scout comes home upset, having been told by Ms. Caroline, her first grade teacher, that she shouldn't be reading at home with her father. Atticus neither dismisses Scout's troubles nor stampedes to the school to blame the teacher. He calmly meets her on the front porch, listens to her concerns, and offers a life lesson on compromise that would serve her well for the rest of her life: "If you'll concede the necessity of going to school, we'll go on reading every night just as we always have. Is it a bargain?"[2]

Atticus is the perfect parent, and it nearly makes me sick. Maybe I'm being too hard on myself. Even before our first child was born, my wife and I began the difficult process of perfect parenting. One pregnancy book would offer advice on what to eat, how to exercise, and what kind of paint to use in the nursery. We thought we were well on our way toward perfection until we picked up another pregnancy book, which completely contradicted the first. And the quest for perfection certainly didn't end when our daughters were born. Now we ask, "Which school is the best?" "Should they start piano lessons or ballet or gymnastics or math club?" "Are their lunches perfectly balanced meals?" "If they get sick, who is the best doctor to use?" And the questions never seem to stop.

You don't have to be a parent to understand the pressure for perfection. There's the anxiety to be the perfect spouse—striving to be patient and kind, never arrogant or rude, believing and bearing all things (see 1 Corinthians 13). There's the stress to be the perfect student—making straight As, graduating debt free, and landing that first job, which sets up your career until retirement before the registrar even puts the diploma in the mail. Do you strive to be the perfect employee who makes all deadlines, cuts expenses, and organizes the company picnic? Or maybe the perfect hipster who only uses a typewriter with handmade paper? Maybe you strive to be the perfect Christian who tithes, serves on the leadership team, stocks shelves in the food pantry, reads Scripture aloud during congregational worship, and chooses the color scheme in the new children's area. Perfection seems to be the goal, but if our own perfection is our ideal, Scripture tells us we are misguided.

In Luke 18, Jesus tells a story of a Pharisee and a tax collector who went to the temple to pray. The Pharisee offered the Lord an explanation of the many ways he was on the way to perfection. He tithed, he fasted, he didn't associate with the riff-raff who panhandled outside the sanctuary. Conversely, the tax collector averted his eyes, beat his chest, and recognized just how far from perfection he really was. Jesus shocks the crowd by saying that it was the tax collector and not the Pharisee who went away justified because the tax collector recognized his imperfections and need for grace.

Jesus continues the lesson later in Luke 18 when a rich young man asks him, " 'Good Teacher, what must I do to obtain eternal life?' Jesus replied, 'Why do you call me good? No one is good except the one God.' " If even Jesus claims he isn't good, then I'm off the hook, right? Jesus is pointing us to the truth that striving for personal perfection isn't required; rather, what we need is the perfecting grace of God.

Maybe perfection itself isn't perfect—maybe it is actually relative. As perfect as Atticus seems to be, his children don't see it. Atticus embarrasses Scout because he's older than other parents, he doesn't hunt, and he's a bit "bookish." As a young girl she doesn't initially understand his role in the community or his encouraging influence to many in town. Over time her opinion of her father changes, just as I imagine your understanding of your own parents changes as you grow and mature. When I was young, my parents were basically superheroes to me. During my teenage years they couldn't have been more embarrassing or lame. In college my relationship with my parents was rooted in laundry, spending money, and weekend groceries. Then, miraculously, when I began having children of my own, my parents once again became superheroes in my eyes.

How has your understanding of your parents changed over time? How has your understanding of our heavenly parent changed through the years? When you were young, did you understand God as an old man with a long beard sitting in the clouds? When people spoke of God as "The Father," did it conjure up images of your own dad? The image of God as Father is certainly appropriate and beautiful and biblical, but it can also be devastating if our earthly fathers were far from being persons of grace or love. I have heard people describe God as "The Perfect Parent," but there's a danger in this. Sometimes we think about God as being human, but better. Some theologians describe this as looking into a well. We think we are seeing God, but we are really looking at a distorted reflection of our self; or as Karl Barth said, "One cannot speak of God simply by speaking of man in a loud voice."[3] So, it's not that God is like my dad—only better—or like an exceedingly benevolent king or like a soldier who wins peace without bloodshed. All these metaphors break down eventually. The good news is that we don't have to guess what God is like. God knew that our human imaginations could only carry us so far, which is why God put on flesh and dwelt among us in the person of Jesus Christ.

Atticus sits on the porch with Scout and asks her if she knows the meaning of compromise. He says that if she concedes the need to go to school that they will continue reading together, just as they always have. If Scout lets go of the desire for radical independence, then their relationship will continue as it always has. God put on flesh and walked among us in order to bring the Law to perfect completion. The covenant established in the person of Jesus Christ is more than a compromise—it is the solution. Jesus takes on our imperfections and transforms them through grace. Christ offers us his love and grace, which leads us in being honest about our shortcomings and seeking forgiveness and reconciliation for our missteps. Conceding the need to rely on our own understanding helps us see that God will always be our God!

Do you feel a pressure for perfection? Have you ever found yourself to actually be perfect?

49

Read the creation account in Genesis 1. How many times is "perfect" mentioned?

Looking back on your life, what are some things you thought were imperfections that turned out to be blessings?

HERO VERSUS SAINT

"Miss Jean Louise, stand up. Your father's passin'."[4]
—Reverend Sykes, to Scout

Atticus Finch is a man of compassion, justice, and courage, but he's no hero. Heroes live for the glory and the honor. Heroes vanquish enemies through strength and power; they live for the battle. Hercules is a hero. Achilles is a hero. Though Atticus is an outstanding fictional model of Christian courage, he's no hero—he's a saint.

The word *hero* rarely appears in Scripture, however *saint* appears sixty-four times in the New Testament. So what's the difference between the hero and the saint? First, there's a difference in the stories they tell.[5] The hero's story is a story in which everything is going poorly, and the hero steps in and makes everything right. In short, the hero's story is about the hero and his or her accomplishments. The saint, on the other hand, is not the center of attention, and doesn't always fix the problem at hand. Atticus steps in to defend Tom Robinson, not because he thinks he's going to win—in fact, he's pretty sure he won't—but because it is the right thing to do. Fundamentally, the hero's story is about the hero. The saint's story is always really a story about God; and in this case, Atticus' story proclaims all are made in the image of God. All deserve compassion, justice, and grace—from the innocent Tom Robinson to malevolent Bob Ewell.

The second distinction between *hero* and *saint* is the question of *why* the story is told. The hero's story is told to celebrate virtues of the hero—the hero's strength or wisdom or sense of timing. The saint's story is told to point out a truth independent of the saint. It seems blasphemous to say but Atticus isn't an excellent lawyer. He could have better challenged Bob Ewell, maybe called an extra witness or two, or pandered to the racism of the day to claim that Tom really didn't know any better. Atticus' strength is not invincibility or superhuman intellect, and he certainly can't leap tall buildings with a single bound. His strength is his faith in knowing that bigotry and hate will not have the final word. Atticus isn't in the courtroom to share his own cleverness; rather, his argument points the audience to a hope that not even Atticus can supply. Although it's not explicit, his strength is in the cross—Jesus accepted the cross, and by accepting death, Christ ensured that death would not have the final answer. It's like taking a case you know you will lose so that injustice will only have one more short-lived victory.

The third difference between the hero and the saint is what the story takes for granted. The hero's story assumes a world in which there will be conflict so that the hero can prove good can prevail. For the hero, conflict is necessary in order for good to defeat evil. The saint's story assumes that nonviolence is the means of communicating the good. There are several occasions in which Atticus meets violence with nonviolence. One of the most tense is when Atticus is sitting outside the jail keeping watch over Tom

Robinson when three cars drive up. They ask Atticus to step out of the way so they can take matters into their own hands. Though Atticus becomes fearful that the situation might get out of hand, he stands his ground and gives the example that courage is not the absence of fear—rather courage is the absence of self. Atticus does not meet the men with violence, but with a rocking chair, a reading lamp, and a newspaper. He offers himself rather than a fight.

In Luke 22, Jesus is being arrested and one of his disciples draws a sword and cuts off the ear of one of the high priest's slaves. Jesus says, "No more of this," and heals the man who had come to capture him (v. 51).

The saint assumes conflict is necessary. The saint does not dismiss violence, but knows it is not the primary means of good. It's an easy thing when a bully is going after you to meet them with a rocking chair, a reading lamp, and a newspaper; but being a father, I cannot promise that I will meet a perpetrator who is going after my children with a newspaper. I live in the hope of resurrection. I offer my life to the kingdom of God without hesitation, but I also feel that we are called to defend those who cannot defend themselves, and this is well represented in this scene; for as Atticus is walking away, a voice from the bushes calls out. Mr. Underwood and his shotgun had been nearby the whole time, ready and waiting to come to his defense.

Finally, the difference between the hero and the saint is what happens when the story goes wrong. If the hero does not succeed, all will be lost. The saint expects failure because success is ultimately God's. Atticus is unsure Tom Robinson's case will be victorious, but he hopes it will be a loss that will shine a powerful light of truth into a dark and systemic issue. As members of the church, we must learn to redefine our understanding of *success*. Success does not mean lots of members and lots of money, although lots of people

A MATTER OF NATIONAL HONOR

In 2007, Harper Lee was awarded America's highest civilian honor, the Presidential Medal of Freedom, for her outstanding contribution to literature, based solely on *To Kill a Mockingbird*.

in ministry and lots of money for missions is not a sign of failure either. Success in the church is ultimately measured by means of transformation and growth: How are lives being changed? How are people growing in their faith and discipleship? How are we growing in our love of God and each other? If the hero fails to gain the trophy, then the season was a failure. The saint celebrates the transformation God is making a reality in the world, regardless whether, by worldly standards, we "win" or "lose." Jesus said, "Don't worry about your life, what you'll eat or what you'll drink, or about your body, what you'll wear" (Matthew 6:25). I would add, "Do not worry about whether you win or lose." The hero worries about these things, but Atticus is no hero.

Who is someone you consider to be a hero? Who do you consider to be a saint?

I've heard it said that the only certainties in life are death and taxes. What do you consider to be certain in life?

How do you decide what is right and what is wrong?

FIGHTING THE GOOD FIGHT

But as for you, man of God, run away from all these things.
Instead, pursue righteousness, holy living, faithfulness, love,
endurance, and gentleness. Compete in the good fight of faith.
— 1 Timothy 6:11–12a

Atticus taught his children that to rely on violence is a childish thing to do—that the world would be better off if folk could just hold it in. When news broke that Atticus was defending Tom Robinson, the community wasn't kind to the Finch family. Some children at school were particularly unkind to Scout, who immediately took to fighting in order to defend her father. When, with clinched fists, Scout asked her father if he in fact defended Negros, to her shock and amazement, Atticus admitted to the very thing she had fought to deny. With great grace and humility, Atticus explained that defending Negros is not only the right thing to do, but that he would lose all credibility as a lawyer and a father should he deny another person the right of a fair trial.

Atticus is committed to fighting the good fight for justice. Following in the footsteps of Christ means that one is committed to discovering ways to put down the sword, to find victory through passion, to trust that only Jesus' blood needs to be shed. Have you ever found yourself fighting for something you later discovered wasn't the right thing to fight about? Fighting the good fight, being committed to goodness without violence requires a definition and a belief. You must discern what is good and believe that what you consider to be good is actually greater than evil.

So what is *good*? Jesus said, "Why do you call me good? No one is good except the one God" (Luke 18:19). Scripture tells us that it's not that God *does* good things; rather that which God does *is good*. Scripture tells us that "God is love" (1 John 4:8); therefore where we find love—in a community of patience and kindness, lacking in envy and arrogance, a community that bears and endures all things—we find God. Unfortunately sin clouds our vision for love, causing our definition of goodness to miss the mark.

Sin is an archer's term. It means "missing the mark." Shooting an arrow and missing the center is what "sinning" means. The word *repent* means "to turn around." What's the worst way to sin? Firing arrows into the crowd behind you, not even remotely aiming for the target. Sinning has no purpose. It wastes arrows and people get hurt. When Jesus says, "Repent, for the kingdom of heaven is at hand" (Matthew 3:2 NASB), he is saying, "Turn around and aim at the target. I'll show you where the target is and how to aim. I'll even keep giving you arrows. All I ask is that you daily aim for the target." Here's the thing—it's a moving target. The target is fixed upon God, but God is alive and dynamic and moving.

Another way to look at it is that God's will is the target. What God desires for us is our life's focus. Jesus took the cross and whittled it down into an endless supply of arrows. The Holy Spirit moves the target to the place where God is calling you. This is why we ask for forgiveness daily. The target has moved. God calls us into new adventures all the time. We need God's guidance and help to fire in the right direction each and every day. "Nothing can separate you from the love of God" (see Romans 8:38) means that the target is always there. Your quiver is never empty. It's just that sometimes we lose our focus, and we begin to drift away from where we should aim our energy and gifts and talents. Fighting the good fight is a daily commitment because the target is fixed upon God's dynamic purpose for us.

Once we have come to a definition of what is good, and what is worth fighting for and aiming for, we must continually remind ourselves that good it is more powerful than evil. Relying on violence as a first resort, defending God as if God is incapable of self-defense, is ultimately a lack of faith. Some would say that we must know evil in order to know good, that we must know pain in order to know peace, or that we must experience darkness in order to know light. This is counter to the biblical narrative.

In the beginning God created light and separated darkness out of it. God did not create light and dark as the poles of a dualistic world. God created light; and when sin gets in the way, we experience darkness. Seeing the world in strict dualism—black and white, us and them, even right and wrong—is the result of us thinking we know better than God, as Adam and Eve did when they ate from the tree of the knowledge of good and evil. (See Genesis 3.) Let's put ourselves in Adam and Eve's shoes for a moment. Before eating the fruit, we clearly see God and that which God provides—the good. Once the fruit is consumed, then we begin to consider evil to be a thing of creation. We begin to "know" good and evil as equal and opposite things. This is not the world God intends. Through that original sin, humanity did not eat from the tree of choice or the tree of sin or the tree of putting things before God—humanity ate from the tree of believing evil to be a thing. As we learn from the Creation story, fundamentally, goodness is something and evil is nothing. Yes, this nothingness (evil) causes real hurt and pain, but until we believe that goodness in and of itself is more powerful than the nothingness of evil, we will continue to think that evil is the means of destroying evil, and nothing can only give birth to nothing.

Atticus takes on Tom's doomed case because he believes that goodness, even in the midst of defeat, is ultimately more powerful than hate. Scripture says, "Pursue righteousness, holy living, faithfulness, love, endurance, and gentleness. Compete in the good fight of faith" (1 Timothy 6:11–12a). When we pursue these things, winning looks like something different. It looks like the cross and an empty tomb. It looks like fighting the good fight.

Do you find the idea of sin as "missing the mark" to be demoralizing or liberating?

What is the "good fight," in the context of your life?

Where do you think God's target is today? Where is God pointing you right now?

WALKING AROUND IN SOMEONE ELSE'S SKIN

"I'm no idealist to believe firmly in the integrity of our courts and in the jury system—that is no ideal to me, it is a living, working reality."[6] —Atticus to the jury

Atticus believes that if a person could just walk around in someone else's skin, he or she would no doubt have a kinder, clearer perspective of the world. In fact, trying to understand the world from another's perspective is arguably the central message of *To Kill a Mockingbird*. Many of the characters in *To Kill a Mockingbird* serve as vehicles through which the reader sees the world from another's perspective. Walter Cunningham drowning his dinner in syrup is a lesson in poverty. Mrs. Dubose's ornery demeanor is a means of understanding the difficulty of dealing with addiction. Tom Robinson's trial is a window into the systematic racism of the Jim Crow South. Even though *To Kill a Mockingbird* is Scout's story, Atticus points us to a story best understood through multiple "skins."

In ninth grade I went on a mission trip with my youth group. We traveled to the hills of Appalachia to help local residents with minor home repairs. One of the homes we worked on was in desperate need of a new roof and foundational support—the house was in disrepair literally from top to bottom. An old man and a dog, the only residents of the home, would come out and sit on the porch and watch us work. Day after day, the man would simply watch us and smile. Late in the week he presented us with a plateful of chicken patties, then headed out to take a walk to the corner store, which was a couple of miles up the holler.

It turned out that the chicken patties were not delicious—in fact, they were so bad that many of us threw them into the woods rather than eat them. We were still hungry, so one of the guys suggested we go into the man's house to look for something else to eat. (Admittedly, not our finest hour.) We got into the house and started looking around, passing through a filthy living room to the kitchen, if you could call it that. I opened the fridge and saw an empty box of chicken patties and nothing else. This man had served us the only food he had, and we were so careless and thankless that we threw it into the woods.

I felt sick. If I had only spent a moment to walk around in this man's skin, I would have recognized the amazing gift he was trying to offer us. For the rest of the trip we remained silent about the whole thing for no other reason than we didn't know what to say. What if he found out? How do you apologize when an "I'm sorry" won't fill someone's empty plate? Maybe he did realize what happened, and walked around in our skin to know that we were stupid teenagers who didn't deserve the kindness of his front-porch smile.

Walking around in someone else's skin—considering the other's point of view—is one of the best ways to resolve conflict. And one of the best ways we can walk around in someone else's skin is through the discipline of listening. When people come to me with a conflict, the first thing I ask them to do is to listen to each other. One person's job is to explain his or her point, and the other person's job is to listen. After the first person is finished, their roles switch. After each person has explained his or her point and listened to the other person, the real work can begin. I ask each person to explain the other's point of view until the other person is satisfied. Then, again, the roles switch. When each person truly feels he or she has been heard, reconciliation can truly begin.

What is your story? How would you tell it? If you were given five minutes to tell who you are without temptation to impress or trawl for sympathy, how would you describe the peaks and valleys of your life? It can be difficult to share with a friend our highs and lows with reckless abandon, and it is even more difficult to share your story with someone who might challenge your self-perception. Several years ago I had the blessing of traveling to Israel for a pilgrimage. Near the end of the tour, our group traveled to Masada, Herod's mountaintop palace, known to be the last Jewish stand against the Roman army during the Jewish Revolt ending in A.D. 70. The museum at the site detailed how the Jewish rebels defied the Roman guard for years before finally committing suicide on the eve of defeat in order to die in freedom rather than live in slavery. Our Palestinian tour guide offered a different story, simply saying, "The rebels didn't die by their own hand, but at the point of a Roman *pugio*. The story of suicide is to change embarrassment to national pride." Which story is correct? I'm convinced the facts of what happened two thousand years ago will never be as important as the meaning behind what Masada represents. To one group it is a symbol meant to inspire resistance against oppression. To another it is a symbol of oppression itself.

The same could be said for the racial and economic tension of our time. Not all black people are wealthy, and not all white people are poor; and if you think you read that sentence backward, the point has already been made. Phrases like "white privilege," "reverse racism," "Black Lives Matter," and "I support the police," conjure up meanings much more powerful than the facts they support. Reconciliation is the fruit of a proclaimed truth—we are all equal and cherished in the sight of God—and something we must cling firmly to, especially when stories and meaning differ.

Atticus believes in the beauty of the justice system, not because it is flawless, but because he believes it is the best environment in which to discover and share truth. In his closing arguments, Atticus shares that all humanity—and not one race in particular—shares immorality. He doesn't claim leniency on the grounds of

SWEET RECOGNITION

The Finches' neighbor Miss Maudie is famous for baking cakes. After Tom's trial, Miss Maudie invites Jem, Scout, and Dill over for a cake baked especially for them, in honor of Atticus' efforts for Tom.

universalism—that because we have all told a lie at one point or another, then no one should be held liable; rather he attempts to chip away at systemic racism on the whole. Fighting the good fight to end racism is what actually causes Atticus to lose the case. If he had pandered to the assumption that Negros are incapable of knowing right and wrong because of their inferior humanity, Tom may have been acquitted. Instead, Atticus fought to challenge people's beliefs so that a new and more hopeful narrative might be born.

If we could just walk around in someone else's skin, we would have a better perspective on truth. The beauty of Atticus' famous phrase is that skin—the color of it, that is—is literally the root of Maycomb's "usual disease" of racism. But if we could change the phrase for us today—if instead of walking around in "someone else's skin," perhaps we should be challenged to walk around in "someone else's economic state"—would that experience alter the way we work toward reconciliation? Or walk around in someone else's gender or orientation or language? Even though Atticus believes the courts are where truth is proclaimed, the church is the place where we celebrate and are challenged by the Incarnation— God putting on skin in order to save the skin we're in. God "put on" humanity so that we might know how to live, and die, so that we might dwell in God's abundant love and offer that love to others.

In whose skin should you spend some time, and who do you wish could take a walk in yours?

How might the experience of considering another's perspective alter the way you see your life and your role in God's story?

the faith of a

Mockingbird

Chapter Three

TOM ROBINSON
WHEN CHALLENGE IS DEFINING

*"There is neither Jew nor Greek; there is neither slave nor
free; nor is there male and female, for you are all one in
Christ Jesus." – Galatians 3:28*

The story Scout tells in *To Kill a Mockingbird* encourages us to
discover our role in God's story; Atticus helps us understand
how to walk in Christ when life becomes challenging and difficult;
and Tom Robinson's plight invites us to consider how difficulty,
hatred, and prejudice can define a person's life. When Paul says
in his letter to the Galatians, "You are all one in Christ Jesus"
(Galatians 3:28), he is not advocating for a colorblind world; rather
he is pointing to a kingdom in which the distinction between "us"
and "them" is broken under the weight of a cross and redeemed
through the empty tomb.

MEET TOM ROBINSON

Tom Robinson is an African American day laborer who lives a quiet life until he is accused of raping Mayella Ewell, a young white woman.

Tom is a longtime member of First Purchase African M.E. Church, and has a wife, Helen, and three children. He is a kind, soft-spoken man, respected by his peers. Tom has one crippled arm, a foot shorter than the other, because it was mangled in a cotton gin when he was a boy. Though seriously injured, Tom had survived and gone on to be able to work to support his family, picking cotton and doing fieldwork for Mr. Link Deas.

A tragic figure, caught in a helpless fate, Tom's trial dominates most of the drama within *To Kill a Mockingbird*, and in doing so, the trial presents a snapshot of injustices that many African Americans experienced during the Jim Crow-era South. Even though Atticus' defense effectively shows that Tom is innocent, and that Mayella's father, Bob Ewell, deliberately and falsely accused Tom, the all-white jury still finds him guilty. Tom's story ends tragically in a barrage of gunfire, as he is murdered during an alleged jail escape. His wife, and the entire Negro community, are devastated, but deeply respect Atticus for what he tried to do for Tom. Many in the white community are also respectful of Tom's memory—including Link Deas, who gives Helen a job so that she help support her family. Tom can be understood as one of the "mockingbirds" in this story—one of those who only offer good, but are ultimately sacrificed on the altar of ignorance and hate.

Talking about race can be difficult for many of us. Each of us comes to the table of reconciliation with our personal narrative and baggage. An African American woman experiences racism differently than does a white male; a black man has a different daily story than does a white woman living in the same town. For some, neither "black" nor "white" labels make sense, never mind how forgetful the mainstream can be about Arab, Asian, Native American, and Latino communities. Not only do each of our personal stories make this discussion difficult, but the issues become more complicated when economic prejudice, cultural stereotypes, and imbalances in civil representation are brought into the conversation.

The conversation about racism and inequality in the United States has certainly changed in the decades since *To Kill a Mockingbird* was published; yet, it is one that is still very timely and extremely relevant to us today. This is why Harper Lee's story— and her character Tom Robinson—is such an important one. Through Tom's story, we are able to clearly see how injustice and prejudice too often color our stories and perceptions, and how that knowledge leaves us no option but to seek Christ and his path of truth and reconciliation.

AN ASSUMED LIFE

"I try to give 'em a reason, you see. It helps folks if they can latch on to a reason."[1] —Mr. Dolphus Raymond

When Tom Robinson, a black man, is accused of raping Mayella Ewell, a white woman, no one seems to think his trial will be anything more than a required formality. As the trial unfolds, the evidence seems to suggest not only that Tom is innocent of the crime, but that Bob Ewell orchestrated the entire affair in order to hide the shame of his daughter's attraction to Tom. Ultimately, the evidence is not strong enough to overcome the jury's assumptions, and Tom is pronounced guilty and led away with little hope of an appeal. In this story, it is easy to see that the sin of prejudice and racism is on the stand in Maycomb, Alabama; but if we look a bit deeper, we will see that *To Kill a Mockingbird* reveals a universal human characteristic that is also on trial—the power of our assumptions.

Each of us brings our own assumptions into the arena of race. Some assumptions are good and maybe even holy, while other assumptions are at best misinformed and at worst hateful. As we've discussed before, by the power of the Holy Spirit, the habits of the church—prayer, fasting, study, covenant groups, communion—transform who we are; and in large part, the transformation that occurs is a transformation of our assumptions. For example, when I was a child, I assumed that the sun went around the earth. It seemed to make sense with my experience—it certainly looked as though the sun rose in one direction and set in another. But through education, my assumptions changed. I now assume that it is the earth that rotates both on its axis and in orbit around the sun. It is still an assumption because it doesn't feel like the earth is moving, nor have I been far enough away to see the earth rotate around the sun, but I trust what I've been taught about the mechanics of our solar system. It's an informed assumption.

Through her novel, Harper Lee cleverly opens our eyes to the power of assumptions. Just before Tom's trial, Scout, Jem, and Dill notice Mr. Dolphus Raymond, a white man who is often seen drinking from a brown paper bag and loitering with Maycomb's black residents outside the courthouse. The town knows Mr. Raymond to be a drunk, and the children are leery about his presence. Near the end of the trial, the children again find Dolphus near the courthouse, and he cordially invites Dill to take sip from his brown paper bag. Dill accepts and is surprised to discover that Dolphus is actually drinking a soft drink—that he's not a drunk after all. The outsider Dolphus, who is married to a black woman and has "mixed" children, pretends to be a drunk so that the town will accept how he can live so counterculturally. We could discuss the tragedy that being a drunk was a better social status than loving a black woman, or that Dolphus found it better to pretend to be someone he wasn't than to own his choices and beliefs. As it was, it seems he assumed he was better off living with the pathetic "Well-he-just-can't-help-it" scorn of the townspeople rather than being ostracized altogether. In truth, the assumptions the community holds about Dolphus and the appearance he projects are accepted as reality, even though both are false.

Have you ever been surprised by the unraveling of your own assumptions? If your ideas about the world, your neighbors, and how God is working in your life and in the world haven't changed in the last few years, then I would gently suggest maybe it's time to look at things in a different way. Maybe it's time to go on retreat, worship at the early service instead of the late one, or take a different route to work. Sometimes it doesn't take much to shake up our assumptions. Other times something more radical is in order—maybe it's time to save up for that mission trip you've been avoiding, start tithing, surround yourself with a community who will fill you with the courage to end an abusive relationship, or walk into that first AA meeting. Maybe it's not your assumptions that need unraveling, but the assumptions you lead others to believe about you. Is there something you keep hidden out of fear of what others might think? Do you hide because you feel others think you vote for the wrong person, love the wrong person, listen to the wrong music, or hang in the wrong places?

Jesus often associated with "undesirables"—fully aware of who they were and confident in who he was: "John the Baptist came neither eating bread nor drinking wine, and you say, 'He has a demon.' Yet the Human One came eating and drinking, and you say, 'Look, a glutton and a drunk, a friend of tax collectors and sinners' " (Luke 7:33–34). When a disreputable woman knelt before Jesus, cleaning his feet with her tears and drying them with her hair, a nearby Pharisee chided to himself that if Jesus really was from God, he would know who this woman was (see Luke 7:36–50). There's a bit of irony here in that the Pharisee assumes that he knows who the woman is and that he knows who Jesus is not. The Pharisee incorrectly assumes that this woman is a sinner, but Jesus sees her true identity as one who is forgiven. "Jesus said to the woman, 'Your faith has saved you. Go in peace' " (Luke 7:50).

Is there something in your soul in need of healing, a secret that's too embarrassing to share? Are you pretending to be an expert at your job so that the promotion will be yours, regardless of what's best for the company? Do you pretend to have it all together at worship so that no one will discover the deep spiritual apathy in your heart? Are you pretending to love your significant other because the wedding has already been planned and it would be too shameful to back out now? Do you assume no one will understand, or that your sin is too great to be forgiven?

STRANGER THAN FICTION

Though not an autobiography, many people, places, and events in *To Kill a Mockingbird* are based on Harper Lee's hometown of Monroeville, Alabama, and the things she experienced growing up there.

Assumptions help us navigate the world around us, but because we are so dependent on them, our false assumptions can cause others great pain. Assuming I can understand an African American woman dealing with racism in America misses the mark. Assuming Tom Robinson is guilty before the trial begins means the trial is a farce. Pretending to be a drunkard out of the shame of loving the "wrong" person is a shackled life. When we in the church say "God knows" or "Jesus understands," we don't mean that there is a great divine eye in the sky watching your every move; rather we proclaim that God's love for you is independent of assumption and supersedes the projections we offer out of fear or shame.

Being in Christ offers us the courage to step outside of our context. Rather than assuming how someone else sees the world, we are called to walk along with others as they live out the unique journeys God has given them. God created us all with great intention and love, and therefore we are called to throw out those assumptions that prevent us from being in community with those of different cultures and creeds. In doing so, we receive a bigger and more beautiful picture of who God is.

What are some of the helpful assumptions you carry with you each day? What assumptions need transformation? How can you know?

What are some ways in which your small group or church can seek diversity?

Who can you invite to your group to help offer a new and different perspective?

THE COLORFUL TABLE

You are all God's children through faith in Christ Jesus. All of you who were baptized into Christ have clothed yourselves with Christ. There is neither Jew nor Greek; there is neither slave nor free; nor is there male and female, for you are all one in Christ Jesus. – Galatians 3:26–28

Finding our place in God's story and honoring each other's place in that story can sometimes be difficult and awkward. Several years ago I had the blessing of hosting Cambodian missionaries for a potluck dinner. In what I'd hoped would be a kind gesture, I planned to greet them using a native greeting. We gathered everyone together, and after thanking everyone for their attendance, I placed my hands together and bowed to them saying, "Namaste." They looked back at me with completely blank expressions. Thinking they might not have heard me, I bowed again toward the missionaries and said, "Namaste," slower and louder. Again, they replied with blank stares.

Now, a reasonable person would have moved on and begun the evening's program, but unfortunately I left my reason at the potluck table somewhere near the fried chicken. So, for the third time, I bowed lower and spoke louder than before. Nothing.

"Don't your people use that word?" I asked. (Yes, I actually said, "Your people." May God forgive me.)

"No. I am not familiar with that greeting," said one of the missionaries.

"It means, 'The Christ in me bows to the Christ in you,'" I said.

"That sounds like a wonderful greeting," she replied.

I later discovered that "Namaste" is Hindu Sanskrit. It's not Cambodian, nor is it Buddhist (the dominant faith tradition in Cambodia). It was as if I'd gone to Canada and greeted everyone with an "Hola, y'all!" It was an epic fail. I assumed they would appreciate the effort I had made to learn something in their language; they probably assumed I was a little crazy.

In order to break down our assumptions about race, sometimes the mantra of being "colorblind," or having the ability to *not* see our differences, is celebrated. If I had seen our Cambodian missionaries simply as missionaries, it would have saved us an awkward, and perhaps offensive, exchange. When we can look beyond race and skin color, we can see people for who they are and not pigeonhole them into predetermined roles we expect them to play. Mayella Ewell has been taught that Tom's skin color means that he is only suited for manual labor, therefore she does not invite Tom Robinson into her home for conversation or a cup of coffee. She doesn't speak with him each day as he walks home from work in order to form a relationship with him. He is invited in only for work—to bust up a chiffarobe, chop firewood, or carry water for her.

Seeing each other as people—rather than black people or white people or, as the song says, "Red and yellow, black and white, they are precious in his sight"—breaks down the assumption that there is an "us" and a "them." What does the color of your skin say about you in the context of your life? Maybe that's a difficult question for you to answer. Let's broaden the question. What do you feel your address or economic situation says about you? What about your choice of where to worship or your denomination?

We have probably all felt stereotyped at some point in our lives, and so we can all understand how throwing away our stereotypes and assumptions can lead us to actually see the people around us as God sees them. Paul writes in Galatians, "You are all God's children through faith in Christ Jesus. All of you who were baptized into Christ have clothed yourselves with Christ. There is neither Jew nor Greek; there is neither slave nor free; nor is there male and female, for you are all one in Christ Jesus" (Galatians 3:26–28). This does not point us to a simple, colorblind, gray society where no individuals exist. There is still Jew, and there is still Greek, but there is no longer Jew *or* Greek. The distinction is very important. There is no more "us versus them." Instead, we are all one in Christ.

It is a bit ironic that the sacraments, or gifts, God offered to the church in order to bring people together are some of the strongest reasons churches have torn each other apart. Every denomination has its own understanding of what happens at baptism, how Christ is present at Holy Communion, and who is welcome to participate. How sweet is it then to know that the Lord's Table is open to all those who are in need of forgiveness and grace and the conviction of the Holy Spirit to grow in love with God. Everyone is invited to the table of God's grace.

Jesus gathered with his disciples on the evening before he was arrested. With him was Simon the Zealot, who wanted to overthrow the government, and Matthew, the tax collector who worked for the government. It was neither political nor fiscal philosophy that brought them together; rather it was Christ who invited them both to share in his ministry. Judas, the betrayer, and Peter, the denier, were also with Jesus at the table. So if a hothead, an office clerk, one who betrays, and one who denies are invited to the table, certainly you and I are welcome as well. This table brings us close to God— a God who walked around in our skin to redeem the skin we're in. It is a table that brings us close to Christ, whose body was broken and raised so that we, who are broken people, might be raised to abundant life. It is a table in which the Holy Spirit fills us with grace and leads us into the hurting places of the world.

We gather around the table as a colorful choir, one body in which every voice is heard for its own beauty, but all voices are directed toward God. It is a place where we become one because there is no Jew or Greek. There is no slave or free. There is no male and female, but we are one in Christ Jesus.

What are the major divisions in your community? Are they racial, political, or economic? All of the above?

How do your roots—your race, your culture, your upbringing—influence your role in God's story? How might he be using you to tell your part of the story?

THE CHOIR AND THE JURY

"Why reasonable people go stark raving mad when anything involving [race] comes up, is something I don't pretend to understand."² – Atticus to Uncle Jack

"All God's creatures have a place in the choir," as the old Bill Staines song reminds us. The question is, who assigns the part and what song does it sing?

Maycomb was certainly divided along racial lines; but on a person-to-person level, people were relatively civil and peaceful to one another. *To Kill a Mockingbird* forces us think about how our social systems work and how people work together within those systems. For example, we can compare two very different groups— the choir members of First Purchase African M.E. Church and the jury members of Tom Robinson's trial.

First, let's consider how a choir does what it does. A choir is a collection of vocalists, each using his or her individual voice for the purpose of sharing music. Individual voices are important, but only as they pertain to the group as a whole. The music isn't always pretty— sometimes discord is purposefully composed into a piece to give it depth and movement. The most important thing is that the individual voices work together as one entity in order to share what the composer has written. There is a beauty in a choir's purposeful unity that goes beyond the composed harmony. Individual voices, each with their own gifts, are all pointed in the same direction, which offers us a model of how we should come together in unity as diverse children of God.

Hearing a choir sing can be a profound spiritual experience if all goes well. On the other hand, it can be a rather hellish experience when a choir isn't unified. A single, overpowering voice can stick out and distract from the harmonies of the whole. Other times the sopranos are flat or the basses forget to count or the altos aren't loud enough. (I believe tenors are a gift from God—they are never wrong.) In these cases, it's easy to know when someone misses the mark, but it is much more difficult to know when the pitch of an a cappella choir as a whole begins to bend. If an a cappella choir begins in the key of F, but through the course of an unaccompanied piece they mistakenly modulate to the key of E, it is nearly impossible to be able to tell that they are no longer singing what the composer intended. Neither the choir nor the audience can immediately tell when the choir is missing the mark. The only person who can really tell is the one with the tuning fork.

Humans have a knack for getting slightly out of tune and veering away from what our Composer intended. This is why systematic racism and prejudice can sometimes be difficult for us to see. If we aren't confronted with these issues in our daily lives, it often becomes hard for us to identify with the injustices of the world. Atticus says to Uncle Jack, "Why reasonable people go stark raving mad when anything involving [race] comes up, is something I don't pretend to understand."[3] Race wasn't a divisive issue for Atticus like it was for many of Maycomb's residents, and so Atticus just couldn't understand their point of view on this issue. If we already consider ourselves "colorblind," we may dismiss or have trouble identifying with the reality of racial tensions that still occur in our country today. For example, a 2004 University of Chicago study revealed that when job applicants submitted resumes with culturally white names, they received 50 percent more callbacks for interviews over those with culturally black names.[4] And in a study

TO THE STARS

For her school Halloween pageant, Scout is dressed as a ham, one of the county's agricultural products. The program is titled "Maycomb County: *Ad Astra Per Aspera*," meaning "Maycomb County: To the Stars Through Difficulties."

that looked at public schools during the 2011–2012 academic year, 74 percent of high schools in which blacks and Latinos make up a majority of the student body offer Algebra II, as opposed to 83 percent of schools in which whites are a majority.[5] Countless studies attest to the racial inequalities that subtly (and maybe not so subtly) exist in our country today—not to mention the studies conducted about gender inequality and the other races that fill America's melting pot.

A choir missing the mark is easy to fix. You stop, wait for the conductor to reestablish the key, and start again. A jury that's missing the mark is much more difficult to discern and even more difficult to correct. A jury's job is almost counter to a choir's job. A choir is given a piece of music with the hope they will sing what is written. A jury is given many notes from many perspectives with the task of putting them together into their version of a song of truth. Individually we can make great strides in reconciling racial tension, but sometimes that can cause us to become blind to the collective bias of our differences on a grand scale.

This is why we need the gospel. The gospel is the piece of music that we are called to sing together. We don't have to guess and barter and weigh truth—instead it is offered to us in the person of Jesus. Even though by definition a jury is never "wrong," Tom's conviction is clearly discordant with the gospel's melody of justice. His story reminds us that every day we must stop, listen to our

Conductor, and sing in tune with God and our neighbor as we work, play, and rest.

What song does your congregation's choir most often sing, and what does it say about your community?

Have you ever served on a jury? Have you ever sung in a choir? What was your experience in each group?

In your city's "choir," which voices are louder than others? How can the justice and mercy within the gospel offer guidance for a more balanced sound?

FEAR OF THE BALCONY

There is no fear in love, but perfect love drives out fear,
because fear expects punishment. The person who is afraid
has not been made perfect in love. – 1 John 4:18

Jem, Scout, and Dill are late in arriving to the courthouse for Tom's trial; and when they arrive, the bottom floor, which is reserved for whites, is standing room only. Reverend Sykes, pastor of First Purchase African M.E. Church, sees that the children are without a seat, and he invites them to sit in the colored balcony. From this vantage point, they can take in the entire courtroom layout—jury over there, Atticus and Tom on one side, the judge in front.

The children's balcony view is a helpful metaphor to consider when looking at the systematic prejudice displayed in *To Kill a Mockingbird*. Up close, you might notice that one of the jurors is a white farmer. Taking a step back, you realize that all of the jury seem to be from the poor white community. Up close, the judge seems casual and relaxed, but from the balcony you can see that he has a tight command of all the courtroom's moving parts.

Taking a step back in order to have a "balcony" perspective gives us a better perspective from which to recognize change. Every now and again, my wife and I will look through vacation photos from years prior. It's fun to see how the children have changed over the years, and it's a bit troubling to see how time seems to be marching all over me. Watching my children grow day to day, it is sometimes difficult to see how they are changing, but looking back at their growth from cooing babies to talkative preschoolers makes me realize just how far they've come. Up close it may be difficult to see the progress, but from the balcony I can see how the pieces are coming together to make them the people God intended them to be.

Sometimes seeing life from the balcony is the best way to fall in love with what God is doing in the world. Think of an impressionist's painting—up close you see only a smudge of color here or a dot of texture there, but stepping back, you'll find a masterwork of beauty that can only be seen from a distance. We can certainly experience God's grace on an intimate level, such as when someone offers forgiveness to another or when disagreements dissolve; but when we ask God to show us the balcony view of how he is working, we begin to see how God is slowly transforming the world into the kingdom of heaven.

Three stories found in Acts 8–9 are great examples of the big picture of God's grace and profound love. The prologue of Acts 8 begins, "On that day [the day Stephen was stoned to death, with the approval of Saul] a severe persecution broke out against the church in Jerusalem, and all except the apostles were scattered throughout the land of Judea and Samaria. Devout men buried Stephen and mourned deeply over him. Saul, however, was ravaging the church. He would enter house after house; drag off men and women, and put them in prison" (vv. 1–3 HCSB). The story begins with Saul persecuting the church and leading Christians into prisons and to the killing fields, but the story is not over yet, and not without hope.

As we continue to read, we see the love of God growing in power and offense. Philip baptizes Simon, who is a Samaritan and therefore an outsider from the Jews, God's chosen people (vv. 9-13). The power of God overflows the walls of Jerusalem, and those outside the Jewish sheepfold are incorporated into the promise of salvation through Christ. A little later in Acts 8, Philip finds himself talking with an Ethiopian eunuch, whom he shares the gospel with and baptizes in a body of water just off the road (vv. 26-38). In this scene God's love has grown from reconciliation of Jew and Gentile to incorporation of a slave, an outcast adopted into God's salvation promise. And then in Acts 9, God's love grows to even more unfathomable heights as Saul, the great terrorist of Christians, is himself confronted by God and converted and becomes Paul, perhaps the greatest theologian Christianity has ever known.

In these passages, God's love brings reconciliation to Jews and Gentiles, and then to those who are neither accepted by Jew or Gentile. God's love triumphs, and God transforms the heart of an enemy into one of the faithful. Each scene communicates a powerful aspect of God's love for humanity—that God desires and offers reconciliation for all—and shows us how God is working through humanity to bring about the kingdom.

It's not just that Jem, Scout, and Dill are in the balcony, but they are in the balcony with "the other," where society says they aren't supposed to be. Might God be calling us into the balcony, where we will worship him alongside other believers who may not think or pray or dress or worship as we do? How we will respond to this call? Will we retreat, in fear of what might happen if we opened our doors to be truly welcoming to anyone who wishes to enter?

Change can be exciting and hopeful, but those of us in the church can fear change. I can only imagine the fear the early church must have felt when they received word that Paul, the church's archenemy and chief persecutor, wanted to come to Jerusalem and preach the good news of Christ. They must have been skeptical, afraid of what might happen next. But God was on the move; and Paul's story, although influential and powerful, was just one of the threads God was using to weave the complete story of his grace. Remembering God's faithfulness, we can trust that he is working in our lives, in our churches, and in our world; and we can live and move in that knowledge confidently because "perfect love drives out fear" (1 John 4:18a).

In what ways is God calling you to open the doors of your home, your church, your community to people who are different from you? How are you responding to his call?

Is it easy or hard for you to live with a "balcony" view of what God is doing in your life? In what areas do you need to ask for God to give you a balcony view?

Falling into Hope

It is a wisdom that none of the present-day rulers have
understood, because if they did understand it, they would
never have crucified the Lord of glory! But this is precisely
what is written: God has prepared things for those who
love him that no eye has seen, or ear has heard, or that
haven't crossed the mind of any human being.
—1 Corinthians 2:8–9

Tom Robinson's story is a difficult account to read and to
process. Even though the prosecution's case has as many holes in it
as a slotted spoon, and Atticus competently argues that Tom could
not have done what he was accused of doing, Tom is convicted
nonetheless. As Tom is led away, Atticus offers a word of hope that
they might have a real chance of acquittal with an appeal, but
Tom barely responds. In the film adaptation of the book, Tom's
hopelessness is evident in this moment. When Atticus speaks to
him, Tom turns only halfway toward Atticus. He remains silent and
dismally turns to leave. One gets the unmistakable sense that Tom is
completely defeated. His challenges have become his identity—the
jury's guilty verdict is not a true statement of his actions, but their
verdict now defines his life, and this destroys him.

Tom's difficult journey ends when, soon after being taken to jail,
he is killed in an alleged attempt to escape. The fact that he was shot
seventeen times only adds to the suspicion that many saw Tom's
fight for justice as a threat to their social system and wanted him

TURNING UP THE HEAT

Unsupervised, Jem once locked a Sunday school classmate in the church furnace room during a game of "Shadrach." The next time Atticus went out of town on a Sunday, Calpurnia took the children to her church.

---

dead, regardless of the truth of his guilt. The abrupt ending to Tom's story was intended to jar us enough to serve as a catalyst for change. It seems that Harper Lee purposely put the period in the wrong place as a means of calling us to complete the story. She seems to ask, "And now what will you do about it?"

Scout helps us to understand what it means to tell a story, and that ultimately we are a part of God's story. Atticus show us what it means for our story to be one of saintly courage devoted to fighting the good fight of the gospel. And Tom reveals that our stories aren't ours alone—we belong to each other. My connection with God is a part of your connection with God. My story is connected to your story. Yes, we are all individually different and beautiful in our own way; but if we are counted as God's children, then our different stories should intersect on the pillars of truth, justice, compassion, and grace.

Take a look at your community. What about it might need to change? What needs to remain lifted up? Creating a diverse community is not about tokenism—seeking the "other" as a means of fulfilling an equation or quota—but calls us to offer the other a voice and a place at the table. It means that we listen to each other's stories. It means learning a new language of sorts, to make an effort of reconciliation, to understand how a community sees and shares the world.

Often the difficult work of reconciliation looks like a defeat. The cross certainly did. When Christ was crucified, it seemed that evil and death had won. It seemed that Jesus must have been little more than a great rabbi, not the great savior his followers had wanted. But those assumptions couldn't have been more wrong. Paul writes:

> "Though he was in the form of God,
>> he did not consider being equal with God something
>> to exploit.
> But he emptied himself
>> by taking the form of a slave
>> and by becoming like human beings.
> When he found himself in the form of a human,
>> he humbled himself by becoming obedient to the
>> point of death,
>> even death on a cross." (Philippians 2:6–8)

> "Because all the fullness of God was pleased to live in him,
>> and he reconciled all things to himself through him—
>> whether things on earth or in the heavens.
> He brought peace through the blood of his cross."
>> (Colossians 1:19–20)

Christ's work on the cross looked like a falling, and it was, but it was a falling into hope. It was an emptying so that we might know the fullness of God. God entered into death in the person of Jesus so that death would no longer have the final world. Christ gave himself so that we might be reconciled to God. What are we being asked to give so that we might be reconciled with each other?

What are some "truths" that we sometimes believe in that don't hold up under the gospel's weight?

Paul says that Christ came in the form of a "slave." How does the picture of Jesus' life change our understanding of social status?

In what areas is God calling for reconciliation in your life and in the life of your community?

Chapter Four

BOO RADLEY
DEFINING A MYSTERY

Listen, I will tell you a mystery! We will not all die, but we will all be changed. – 1 Corinthians 15:51 (NRSV)

*M*ystery can at once be both inviting and terrifying. The unknown can fill us with a sense of adventure and a desire to discover, or it can leave us paralyzed with a fearful inability to see our next step.

One of the most mysterious and haunting questions in all of American literature has to be "Who is Boo Radley?" Throughout *To Kill a Mockingbird,* his identity is a closely guarded secret, and Jem and Scout aren't sure if he's a phantom or a ghost or if he even exists at all. This mystery fuels their curiosity, not only about Boo but about the other mysteries in their world, and opens their eyes to the fact that things are not always as defined or as simple as the citizens of Maycomb would have them believe.

85

Meet Boo Radley

Arthur "Boo" Radley is the mysterious, unknown figure in *To Kill a Mockingbird*. He hasn't been seen outside of the Radley home in years, which spawns rumors among the children that he is a menacing, fanged phantom, responsible for any number of unexplained happenings in town. Outside of Tom Robinson's trial, the children's efforts to discover Boo's identity comprise the majority of the novel's plotline.

According to the neighborhood legend, the Radley family— Mr. and Mrs. Radley and their two sons—had always kept to themselves, rarely participating in the town's social life. As a teenager, their younger son, Arthur, got involved with the wrong crowd, which caused minor mayhem in the town. The presiding judge wanted to send all the boys to the state industrial school to be "reformed," but Mr. Radley refused and pledged to take care of his own son. The doors of the Radley home were shut, and Arthur was hardly ever seen again. Jem imagines that Mr. Radley has Boo chained to his bed, but Atticus remarks that there are other ways to turn someone into a ghost. After Mr. Radley's death, the older son, Mr. Nathan Radley, came home to take his place, and still "Boo" never emerged.

Living three doors down from the Radley place and never knowing any of its secrets is almost more than Jem and Scout can bear, so along with their friend Dill, the children get increasingly brave in their unsuccessful efforts to draw Boo out of the house during their summer breaks. Eventually the children discover that Boo isn't menacing at all; rather, he is one of the gentle "mockingbirds" they are called to protect.

Many stories circulate about Boo, but Jem, Scout, and Dill are not satisfied with Boo as the shadowy protagonist of fireside legends. Instead, they seek to draw him out. When they begin to notice trinkets placed in the knothole of the Radley tree, they think the items are there by mistake or that they have found someone's secret hiding place. Soon they realize these gifts are no accident, but Boo's unique way of communicating with them.

When the children begin to experience Boo firsthand, mystery and misunderstanding give way to a peaceful grace. They realize that while they had been trying to draw Boo out, Boo had been watching over them, making his presence known through gifts— the gifts in the tree, mended and folded pants, a blanket offered on a cold night, and ultimately, the gift of life.

For Jem and Scout, trusting in their curiosity and courage leads them to seek an answer to the question, "Who is Boo Radley?" and it is the very thing that saves their lives.

WHO IS BOO RADLEY?

"Jean Louise, this is Mr. Arthur Radley. I believe he already knows you."[1] *—Atticus to Scout*

Stories are how we make sense of the world. Imagine trying to tell someone about your day without using any stories. Imagine a wedding rehearsal dinner or a graduation reception or a funeral without stories. Stories help us communicate our greatest joys, our deepest fears, and our mournful laments. They help us answer the big questions: Who am I? Where did I come from? Where am I supposed to be going? What is my purpose?

At the heart of *To Kill a Mockingbird* is the haunting question, "Who is Boo Radley?" The children of Maycomb have some wild ideas about Boo Radley. Some say he eats squirrels and watches people during the night, that he has sunken cheeks and large fangs, and that his preferred weapon is a pair of old scissors. Even the adults in town get in on the stories, supporting the children's fantasies that within the Radley house lives a mysterious, dangerous, indefinable phantom.

The question, "Who is Boo Radley?" is not unlike the question, "Who is God?" How do you describe God? Is your description of the divine rooted in big words like *almighty, all-knowing, eternal,* and *everlasting*? Or maybe your understanding of God is understood in the still small voice of an intimate friend or compassionate parent. In my first year of seminary, we students tried to learn everything we could about God. In essence, we were taught to fill our "God Box." The problem was, after the first year of seminary, there was the temptation to think that I had learned all I needed to know about God—little did I know that the two remaining years of seminary would be all about unpacking the box I had built. Sometimes we can fall into the trap that we have learned all we need to know about God, but if we stop at a definition of God, then we leave no room for growth or relationship. When Moses asks the voice from the burning bush, "What is your name? Who is it that is sending me to Pharaoh?" YHWY replies, "I Am Who I Am" (Exodus 3:13–14). In other words, Moses is seeking a definition, but God offers an experience.

The adults of Maycomb have defined everyone and everything. Everyone fits neatly into his or her own box—the Ewells are trash, the Cunninghams will always be poor, and Tom Robinson is black and therefore guilty. Everyone has been weighed and measured for good or ill for a place in society. Boo Radley doesn't fit into any of the preconceived categories laid out for the townspeople; therefore folk don't know what to do with him. Scout is another person who doesn't fit squarely into Maycomb's categories, so perhaps she feels a kinship with Boo, and her curiosity will not allow Boo to remain a mystery for long. She wants to know him and experience him.

Do you long to know and experience God? How is it that you connect with him? Do you see God in nature? Do you mainly see God through relationship with one another? Maybe you struggle to experience God on a daily basis. If so, try this: think of God as being in an eternal "now." He is always present and never exhausted. He can speak through someone's kind words to you today just as he can speak through ancient Scripture. And even though there will always be mystery surrounding God and who he is, faith in God offers a kind of holy peace with mystery. When I was a child, what I knew about my father's day was that he left for work in the morning and came home before supper in the evening. I knew that he was a chemist and that he worked for a paint company, but at the time I really didn't know what that meant, nor did it particularly matter. I knew who my dad was in my eyes—a thoughtful, loving, and joyful man who took care of our family and who was a faithful servant of our church and took seriously Christ's commandment to love one's neighbor. I didn't need to know all the particulars about what my dad did during the day; I trusted my experience of who I knew him to be in order to shape my faith in him.

Saint Anselm, an 11th century Benedictine monk, was said to live by the motto, "Faith seeking understanding." Our faith in God, our trust that God will fulfill his promises, grows with our understanding of God. Faith inspires understanding, and understanding

HIDDEN TALENT

Atticus is considered the best shot in Maycomb County, though his children have no idea of his talent until the day he has to shoot a rabid dog that is wandering through the neighborhood.

---

inspires faith. Our belief in God calls us into a deeper understanding of who God is, and as we continue to discover how God is working in and through the world, our faith matures and is strengthened. This doesn't mean we will ever have God "figured out," so to speak. Faith not only keeps us connected to God but also strengthens our trust in God even when we don't understand. Some aspects of who God is will always remain a mystery to us, and that's okay! As Scout begins to realize more about Boo, that he was the one offering gifts in the knothole of the tree and was the one who comforted her during Ms. Maudie's fire, the fear of mystery dissipates.

How do we describe the seemingly indescribable? Who *is* God? God is not simply the main character of ancient stories. God is calling us out to seek and to find the life that he has prepared for us through Christ in the power of the Holy Spirit. Whether it is faith seeking understanding or if it is understanding seeking faith, the point is to *seek*. Scout, Jem, and Dill refuse to allow Boo to remain a mystery, and in their seeking they discover that the indescribable is not nearly as frightening as they had imagined.

Are you curious about God? In what ways do you desire to know more about God?

How do you most often experience God? What times or experiences open you up to better hear the divine voice?

FROM STORY TO COMMUNION

On the day the LORD God made earth and sky—before any
wild plants appeared on the earth, and before any field crops
grew, because the LORD God hadn't yet sent rain on the
earth and there was still no human being to farm the fertile
land, though a stream rose from the earth and watered all
of the fertile land—the LORD God formed the human from
the topsoil of the fertile land and blew life's breath into his
nostrils. The human came to life. – Genesis 2:4–7

The story of our Christian faith is a most beautiful one, found in the holy library we call the Bible. This story narrates the truth of the heart of God, and of our hearts, and how we are wonderfully connected to God.

The story begins where it should—in the beginning. God looked upon the dark void and filled it with light, and near the end of six periods of creative fervor, God created humanity; and our story with God begins—Adam and Eve, Noah and the ark, Moses and the Exodus, David and the kingdom of Israel, Jesus and the kingdom of God, the apostles and the church ... and you! We don't make sense without the full story, but our relationship with God and each other doesn't end there—story becomes practice.

Jem, Scout, and Dill spend most of the summer playing a game they call "Boo Radley." Scout plays Mrs. Radley, Dill is Mr. Radley, and, being the one who actually survived after sneaking up to and touching the Radley house, Jem gets to play to Boo. On the front

91

lawn, the children begin to act out stories they have heard told about the tragic family, and as the summer progresses, their story becomes more detailed and imaginative. They began to add characters to the drama, developing a whole new story of their own.

Story becomes practice. Who we are and where we've been become our practice, our culture and tradition. In the church our story is the word of God, and the practice of that story is worship and service. We gather to hear holy stories. We lift our hands to sing the songs of our faith. We are sent out into the world for service. This word becomes the focus of prayer and the heart of our mission. We go out into the world to serve, not because it is a good idea or because it is helpful or makes good economic sense. We go to serve because it puts the Word of God into practice. Jem, Scout, and Dill are not satisfied with Boo remaining a legend. They know what the townspeople say about Boo, but they'd rather seek him out for themselves.

God is not to remain the protagonist of our bedtime stories. Through worship and practice God is calling us out to seek the kingdom, which Jesus compared to a mustard seed—beautiful, life giving, but terribly overlooked. The kingdom of God is the place where the poor are welcomed, the meek receive inheritance, and peacemakers see God's face. Jesus describes this kingdom as a mustard seed, a treasure, and a pearl, suggesting not only that the kingdom is easily missed but that it is precious. The mustard seed, treasure, and pearl are also all born out of darkness. The seed must be planted in the earth in order to bring forth life. The treasure is buried in a field in order to be exhumed in glory. The pearl is formed from an irritating grain of sand hidden in the darkness of an ocean-covered oyster. The kingdom is God's presence fully realized in Jesus' life, suffering, death, and resurrection. In our seeking, in our practice and worship, we participate in Jesus' life, which brings us into connection with God's saving grace.

It isn't long after their "play" ends that the children start back to school and begin to notice random little trinkets in the knothole of the Radley tree—chewing gum, grey twine, two dolls made of soap, a medal, a broken watch, and two copper pennies. One day Jem and Scout find two soap carvings of themselves in the tree— their rudimentary shapes curiously intimate and thoughtful. It then becomes apparent that someone in the Radley house is trying to reach out to them in small but meaningful ways. The legend (Boo) was becoming real and reaching out to them, communicating with them. The stories they heard were put into practice, and now their practice has become communication. The gifts Boo offers are a sign to the children that Boo has noticed their summer games.

Scripture tells in Genesis 2:7 how God created a human from the dirt of the ground—how he took a common thing (dirt) one might sweep away—and from it created a beautiful and enduring connection. In our spiritual practice, God's word becomes worship, and worship becomes communion with him. God's revelation in Scripture is lived out in worship and service, and our worship and service bring us into communion with God and with each other. In many denominations this communion with God and neighbor is simply called "Communion." Some gather around an altar where the essence of bread and wine become the broken body and shed blood of Christ. Others pass bread and juice within the pews in remembrance of Christ, recognizing the importance of community. Others kneel in prayer near the Lord's Table, where in the receiving of the bread and juice in the power of the Holy Spirit, they receive the real presence of Christ. Whether people gather daily or quarterly, or whether one understands that the bread has changed or our remembrance of Christ makes the bread significant, God's word becomes our worship and our worship becomes our communion with God and each other.

When we gather together around the table, we receive nourishment from one loaf of bread, revealing to us that though we are many, we are all one in Christ. Over time, gathering together as one body begins to broaden our vision of those whom God calls as his children. The practice of Communion changes how we see the world and the creator of it.

How does your community celebrate Communion? How does your practice of Communion reveal your understanding of God?

If you could summarize your worship experience into a one-sentence story, what would that story be?

Story leads to practice, practice to communication, and communication to connection. How have you experienced this progression in your relationship with God?

MISUNDERSTOOD

> *"Jem gave a reasonable description of Boo: Boo was about six-and-a-half feet tall, . . . he dined on squirrels. . . . There was a long jagged scar that ran across his face; . . . and he drooled most of the time."*[2]

For most of *To Kill a Mockingbird*, Boo Radley remains hidden from sight. The children have never laid eyes on him, so he is a complete mystery to them. Though there are countless stories and myths about him floating around Maycomb, Boo remains a tragic character that no one seems to understand. And Boo is a mystery to us as well. Harper Lee never lets the readers in on Boo's true story, so we are left to make our own conclusions and opinions about Boo's reclusive behavior.

When dealing with the abstract—such as art or literature—it's sometimes difficult to agree on meaning. The Bible, God's word, is the primary means by which we learn God's story and the role we play within it, and because it is such an important resource for us, there are often disagreements among believers about what God is actually saying in its pages. It seems as though, when it comes to reading Scripture, we are all literalists differently.

Scripture isn't easy to understand, and in order to read and comprehend it well, we must first clear four hurdles that often get in the way of our understanding. First, Scripture is thousands of years old, and, second, it was written in a different language. It is hard enough to understand words within the English tradition that have fallen out of use like *brume*, meaning "mist," or *delitescent*, meaning "hidden," let alone understand these ancient words that were first offered around campfires generations upon generations ago. Time is a large hurdle to overcome, but making matters more difficult is language. English was not the Bible's original language—the Old Testament was originally written in Hebrew, and the New Testament was originally copied in Greek (or Aramaic). Even if the Bible were written completely in contemporary English, there would be misunderstandings. Throw in hundreds of years and many different languages, and the stage is certainly set for misunderstandings.

Several years ago I was on a home repair mission team with some folk from Wisconsin. At the beginning of the workday, I noticed that people had filled up their water bottles, so I asked someone where the water fountain was.

"There are no water fountains here, but the bubbler is in the cafeteria," was the reply.

"What the heck is a bubbler?" I asked.

She said that a bubbler was that thing in the hallway of a school where you push down a button and water comes out. I informed her that to which she was referring was a water fountain.

"No, water fountains are outside large buildings," she said. "Water fountains usually have statues in them."

This is why I never studied Greek. English is hard enough.

The next hurdle we have to overcome when understanding Scripture is culture and the way it affects language. Biblical culture in the Old and New Testaments reflects the lifestyles and worldview of a people living primarily around the eastern Mediterranean region. Culture dictates the meanings of words or phrases, and therefore the same terms can mean different things in different places. For example, if you order "tea" in southern Louisiana, it will be unsweetened iced tea. In northern Louisiana, it will be sweetened with sugar. In neither case will you receive hot tea. In Scripture Jesus tells parables about "talents" in Matthew 18:23–35 and Matthew 25:14–30. Today we think of *talent* as a gift or a special attribute, but a *talent* during Jesus' time refers to a ridiculous amount of money—the exact value is debatable, but we know that one talent was worth many years' worth of wages (so the debtor Jesus references in Matthew 25 who owed his king 10,000 talents was in an absurd amount of debt). In these parables, Jesus wasn't talking about the ability to play the piano or start a puppet ministry, but something amazingly costly.

In addition to time, language, and culture, when reading Scripture we must understand that words in and of themselves are symbols that point to a meaning beyond the actual combination of letters. The meaning of words is dictated by their context, which is the fourth hurdle to overcome when trying to understand Scripture.

What's in a Name?

Calpurnia's church, First Purchase African M.E. Church, was named after its founders—freed slaves who used their first earnings to pay for it. It is the only church in town to have a steeple and bell.

For instance, when you read the word *duck,* do you imagine a bird or someone dodging a falling object? Both definitions are true, depending on the context of the words surrounding *duck.* Without context it is difficult to agree on the simplest of things, which is the main reason Boo is such a mystery to the children. They have no context for who Boo really is. Though they've seen Boo's house, they've never seen Boo. Though they've heard about him, they've never heard *from* him. Or so they think.

Because our relationship with God is rooted primarily in faith of his written word, misunderstandings and disagreements are bound to happen. Sometimes Scripture itself can seem quite clear, but is interpreted in more than one way. In 2 Samuel 7:7 (NRSV), God says to King David through the prophet Nathan, "Wherever I have moved about among all the people of Israel, did I ever speak a word with any of the tribal leaders of Israel, whom I commanded to shepherd my people Israel, saying, 'Why have you not built me a house of cedar?'" Some read this as God desiring a temple. Another way to read it is that God did not want a temple at all: "Are you the one who is going to mess this up by trying to contain me in the walls of the holy of holies?" Listen to what God says earlier in the text—"I haven't lived in a temple from the day I brought Israel out of Egypt until now. Instead, I have been traveling around in a tent and in a dwelling. Throughout my traveling around with the Israelites, did I ever ask Israel's tribal leaders I appointed to

97

shepherd my people: Why haven't you built me a cedar temple?" (7:6–7). In other words, "David, I didn't ask for a temple." So which is it? Does God want a temple or does God not want a temple? Some would argue that Jesus is God's temple, turning the discussion in yet another direction. You can see how things can get confusing.

In reading Scripture we must wrestle with time, language, culture, and context in order to find meaning, which is why meaning must be found within the covenant of relationship with God. The Holy Spirit is the author of meaning, and the Holy Spirit moves around us, through us, and in many cases in spite of us.

Yes, when we read Scripture together there will be disagreements of interpretation. Some will be more significant than others. Scripture is best read in the context of community with other believers, yet pastors do not hold a monopoly on meaning. Neither do leaders in the church. In most cases, it's okay to disagree. When you are in love with a God who is mysterious, it's okay to leave some things unfinished, as it were, because dwelling on the disagreements leaves us only with rubble. When Ms. Maudie's house was on fire, Scout was too busy watching the house burn to realize that Boo had come out of the house to place a blanket on her shoulders to protect her from the bitter cold. How often do we prefer to watch the world burn rather than recognize the grace around us?

Where there is mystery there will be misunderstanding. Thankfully, we are not asked to rely on our own understanding, but to rest in God's grace.

> "Trust in the LORD with all your heart;
>> don't rely on your own intelligence.
> Know him in all your paths,
>> and he will keep your ways straight" (Proverbs 3:5–6).

Read 2 Timothy 3:16. How does this verse inform our understanding of Scripture in the midst of changing culture and context?

Do you find it hard to connect with Scripture? Why or why not?

Read Psalm 23 in different translations. Which translation speaks to you? Why?

GRACE UPON GRACE

We love because God first loved us. – 1 John 4:19

Throughout *To Kill a Mockingbird,* the character of Boo Radley represents God's prevenient grace—the grace that moves toward us before we move toward God.

Prevenient grace means that God loves us even before we know who God is. A good parent or guardian will love a baby, provide for a baby, and care for a baby long before the baby can ever ask for love or nourishment or comfort. If one waited for a baby to ask, "May I have some milk, please?" the child would never survive infancy. Just as we give our children names and lovingly call them by their names long before they can comprehend what we're saying, God calls us by name long before we are ever able to articulate it for ourselves. God's prevenient grace is how we know our identity as children of God, and how we know what love is. "We love because God first loved us" (1 John 4:19). God's work in the world is our definition of love; therefore love must first originate with God.

As the children's summer ends and Dill prepares to leave for home, they muster the courage to peek into the Radley house for a good look at Boo. Jem and Dill slowly creep onto the back porch, leaving Scout behind as a lookout. As they get closer to the window, a shadow crosses their path, leaving them momentarily frozen before they run for it. A shotgun blast rings out in warning, and in the confusion and hurry, Jem gets his pants stuck on the Radley fence. Rather than wiggle his pants free, he jumps out of them, leaving them behind. In one of the book's funniest moments, Jem arrives home in only his underpants, "before God and everyone," as Scout recalls. Atticus asks where Jem's pants have gone, and Jem has the audacity to answer with a bewildered look that all parents and schoolteachers will no doubt recognize. Dill quickly replies that he won them in a game of strip poker, which temporarily gets them off the hook, but really convinces no one. Jem knows he has to get his pants back, but that means going back to the Radley house.

When Jem returns later that evening to retrieve his pants, he finds that they have been neatly folded and mended and laid across the fence. It takes Jem about a week to mull over this discovery before he is able to share his thoughts with Scout. He just can't get over the thought that, somehow, someone knew he would come back for the pants, and that someone in that house had noticed him and was looking out for him. In the next moment, as they are walking past the Radley tree, they notice a ball of gray twine sitting in the knothole of the Radley's tree, almost as if to say, "You're welcome."

Jem's mended pants remind me of the Lord's reaction to the man and the woman in the Genesis story commonly known as "The Fall" (see Genesis 3). Both the man and the woman eat of the fruit of "the tree of the knowledge of good and evil," which God has explicitly told them not to do, and they hide from God because they find that they are naked and exposed in their sin. After the

Lord proclaims the consequences of their disobedience, he fashions clothing for them, like Boo folding and mending Jem's pants. "The Fall" shows us that, even in the midst of disobedience, God is still loving and faithful, knowing what we need and offering it to us.

Mended pants and a ball of twine aren't the only gifts Boo shares with the children. Time and time again the children find gifts in the tree—gum, pennies, soap dolls, a medal, and a watch. Individually the gifts aren't significant, but taken as a whole they are a constant reminder that Boo is watching over them, so to speak. I wonder what kind of gifts God leaves for us each and every day that go relatively unnoticed by us? God is always providing for us and always calling out to us. God's grace is the answer to our daily petition in the Lord's Prayer: "Give us this day our daily bread."

Grace goes before us, works for us, and works within us. There are three complimentary ways of understanding God's grace—prevenient, justifying, and sanctifying. Imagine that you've been given a gift. You're not sure when the gift was delivered to your home, but you notice a box outside your front door. This gift is like God's prevenient grace: You did nothing to earn it. You didn't buy it. It's simply offered to you. Unfortunately this gift is so ubiquitous that it often goes unnoticed. (How long was Boo leaving gifts for the children or for the rest of Maycomb before anyone noticed?) This is when God's work in the person of Jesus Christ enters the story. Christ fashioned the gift before it was delivered; and because it is Christ's gift to offer, Jesus rings the doorbell, showing us where the gift is, and opens the door allowing us access to the gift. This is God's justifying grace—God's work through Jesus' life, death, suffering, and resurrection. Jesus shows us how to live and how to die so that we might live abundantly with God both now and for eternity.

God offers the gift and Jesus shows us the way, but God isn't finished yet. Imagine that you open the gift, and inside you find

Boo Who?

Harper Lee never tells us who gave Boo his nickname, but it seems as though the children are the only ones who ever use the moniker.

---

a musical instrument. Jesus teaches us how to play, and the Holy Spirit guides our daily practice. Eventually, through daily practice empowered by the Spirit's guidance—sanctifying grace—we both learn how to play the music Jesus offers as well as make and share our own compositions.

Boo leaves the children gifts. He covers a preoccupied Scout with a blanket on a cold winter's night. He watches over the children as a loving protector and friend, even as they are ignorant of all that he is doing. God walks with us each and every day whether we acknowledge it or not. God's precious grace goes before us, works for us, and works within us. Even when we turn away, God's love remains steadfast. Grace can often go unnoticed, until we are able to look back and realize those moments in which God's grace was the very thing that saved us.

How do you describe God's grace? What does it mean to you that grace is a gift?

In what ways do you share grace with your friends, family, and those with whom you disagree?

SAVING A LIFE

The light shines in the darkness,
and the darkness doesn't extinguish the light. —John 1:5

Boo Radley hides in the shadows for most of *To Kill a Mockingbird*, until one late October night when Scout finally meets him face-to-face. As Jem and Scout walk home from an evening school program, they realize they are being followed. Thinking that their schoolmate Cecil Jacobs is playing a prank on them, they think little of it until the figure gets closer and Jem shouts for Scout to run. They are attacked not far from the Radley home. During the skirmish Jem is injured, and Scout is left confused and scared. She finds a man lying on the ground and then sees another carrying Jem back to their home.

As Dr. Reynolds tends to Jem's broken arm, the sheriff arrives to tell Atticus that Bob Ewell has been found dead at the site of the attack with a knife lodged in his ribcage. Knowing that neither of the children were carrying a knife, Sheriff Tate asks Scout what happened. After reporting what little she knew, she notices a man standing in the corner of Jem's bedroom and recognizes him as the stranger who carried Jem back to the house. Within a few moments she realizes just who it is that's standing in the corner, and the mystery becomes a reality. In what I believe is one of the finest moments in American cinema, in the film version Scout looks into the man's eyes and says, "Hey, Boo."

To Kill a Mockingbird is framed within brokenness, as is our Christian story. Jem's broken arm is how the story begins and ends, just like our Christian journey finds its center in Jesus' death and resurrection. Boo Radley helps us understand that even in the midst of misunderstanding, even when the ugliness of the world seems to triumph, even when grace goes unnoticed, even in the midst of death, we can find life. This is the central message of Jesus' crucifixion and resurrection.

Jesus accepted the cross, took on humanity's sin, and was buried in a garden tomb outside the walls of Jerusalem, the city of peace. Of course the story doesn't end there. On the third day Jesus rose from the grave, proving God's word of love and justice to be true. What do you suppose the Resurrection looked like? For a long time the picture I held in my head was of the women walking to the tomb on a nice spring day. I imagined the birds chirping, the sun shining, the orchestra in the background playing Grieg's "Morning" movement (*Peer Gynt Suite 1, Opus 46*).

I really love how the Gospel of John remembers the Resurrection because it is so counter to my imagination. John records, "Early in the morning of the first day of the week, while it was still dark, Mary Magdalene came to the tomb and saw that the stone had been taken away from the tomb" (John 20:1). Did you catch that? "While it was still dark," Mary saw that the tomb was empty. Jesus was resurrected in the midst of darkness. The same happens later in the day. Jesus appears before the disciples in the evening (John 20:19). The resurrected Christ appears in the midst of darkness. Suddenly the beginning of John's Gospel makes sense—

> In the beginning was the Word
> > and the Word was with God
> > and the Word was God. . . .
> What came into being
> > through the Word was life,
> > > and the life was the light for all people.

> The light shines in the darkness,
>> and the darkness doesn't extinguish the light.
>>> (John 1:1, 3c–5).

Jesus accepted the cross, but transformed it from a symbol of death to a symbol of light. The gospel is the proclamation that darkness indeed is not as powerful as the light!

Boo Radley hides in Maycomb's shadows, but he is the light that saves the children from Bob Ewell's anger and hate. As Atticus and Sheriff Tate talk about how to reconcile the evening's events, Atticus' legal mind begins to think of when to file what and which court will hear what testimony. Sheriff Tate goes to great lengths to convince him that Bob Ewell fell on his own knife, which would exonerate anyone from having committed a crime. Everyone knows this isn't the truth—though not explicitly mentioned, it seems it was Boo who killed Bob Ewell while defending the children. Mirroring Jesus' words from Luke 9, Sheriff Tate says, "There's a black boy dead for no reason, and the man responsible for it's dead. Let the dead bury the dead this time, Mr. Finch." He continues, "Draggin' [Arthur] with his shy ways into the limelight—to me, that's a sin." Atticus turns to Scout, hoping that she understands, to which she wisely replies, "It'd be sort of be like shooting a mockingbird, wouldn't it?" Atticus turns to Boo and simply says, "Thank you for my children, Arthur."[3]

Christ is the light that shines in the darkness, and the darkness does not overcome it. The gospel doesn't shield us from the ugliness of the world—the prejudice, the hate, the overbearing systems of the world that make justice a difficult reality—but the gospel, the grace of Jesus Christ giving us access to the love of God, is truly all we need to dispel the darkness and transform death into life.

Have you ever considered that Jesus was resurrected in the midst of darkness? What does that mean to you?

Who do you think is the mockingbird of this novel? Is there more than one?

How have you experienced God's life-saving power in your life?

NOTES

CHAPTER ONE – SCOUT FINCH: TELLING YOUR STORY

1. Harper Lee, *To Kill a Mockingbird* (New York: Grand Central Publishing, 1960), chapter 1, page 1.
2. For more on this, check out Andy Crouch's *Culture Making: Recovering Our Creative Calling* (Downer's Grove, IL: InterVarsity Press, 2013).
3. Lee, chapter 14, page 180.
4. Lee, chapter 11, page 149.

CHAPTER TWO – ATTICUS FINCH: WHEN YOUR STORY IS CHALLENGED

1. Harper Lee, *To Kill a Mockingbird* (New York: Grand Central Publishing, 1960), chapter 11, page 133-34.
2. Ibid., chapter 3, page 41.
3. Karl Barth, *The Word of God and the Word of Man* (New York: Harper Torchbooks, 1957), 195.
4. Lee, chapter 21, page 283.
5. The five differences between saints and heroes are outlined in Sam Wells's book *Improvisation: The Drama of Christian Ethics* (Grand Rapids, MI.: Brazos Press, 2004), 42–44.
6. Lee, chapter 20, pages 274.

CHAPTER THREE – TOM ROBINSON: WHEN CHALLENGE IS DEFINING

1. Harper Lee, *To Kill a Mockingbird* (New York: Grand Central Publishing, 1960), chapter 20, page 268.
2. Lee, chapter 9, page 117.
3. Ibid.
4. Marianne Bertrand, "Are Emily and Brendan More Employable than Lakisha and Jamal?" *Capital Ideas* 4, no. 3 (Spring 2003), http://www.chicagobooth.edu/capideas/spring03/racialbias.html.
5. U.S. Department of Education, Office for Civil Rights, *Civil Rights Data Collection: 2011–12,* "Data Snapshot: College and Career Readiness" (March 2014), http://www2.ed.gov/about/offices/list/ocr/docs/crdc-college-and-career-readiness-snapshot.pdf.

CHAPTER FOUR – BOO RADLEY: DEFINING A MYSTERY

1. Harper Lee, *To Kill a Mockingbird* (New York: Grand Central Publishing, 1960), chapter 30, page 363.
2. Lee, chapter 1, page 16.
3. Lee, chapter 30, page 369-70.

ACKNOWLEDGMENTS

I am so thankful to share this study with you, but this study would not have happened without some very special people. I first have to thank my wife, Christie, and my lovely daughters Isabelle, Annaleigh, and Cecilia for sharing me with the ministry in general and this study in particular. I have also been blessed with a loving and supportive family: Thank you to all of the Rawles, Zeringues, Karams, Hinsons, and Thomases.

I must also lift up my colleagues in ministry and the churches I have served. Thank you Reverend Ken Irby, Reverend Dr. James C. Howell, and Reverend Dr. Sam Wells for your patience and grace. I am grateful for Angie Cason, Jasper Peters, and Sabrina Short for helping me think outside of my context. I must acknowledge the support of my colleagues in the Louisiana Conference of The United Methodist Church and the grace I have received from the churches I have served.

I am so thankful to Abingdon Press for offering me this opportunity. To the team: Susan Salley, Ron Kidd, Alan Vermilye, Tim Cobb, Marcia Myatt, Tracey Craddock, Camilla Myers, Sally Sharpe, Sonia Worsham, and Nancy Provost. I also must lift up Lori Jones for making me sound better than I deserve—you have a gift, my friend.